MW00980411

A CIVILIZED
REVOLUTION

A CIVILIZED
REVOLUTION:

MEETING TOMORROW'S CHALLENGE WITH THE PROGRESSIVE DEMOCRATIC ALLIANCE

BY GORDON WILSON

RONSDALE PRESS
1996

A CIVILIZED REVOLUTION
copyright © 1996 Gordon Wilson

All rights reserved. The use of any part of this publication reproduced, transmitted in any form or by any means, electronic, mechanical, photocopying, recording, or otherwise stored in a retrieval system, without the prior consent of the publisher, is an infringement of the copyright law.

RONSDALE PRESS LTD.
3350 West 21st Avenue
Vancouver, B.C., Canada
V6S 1G7

Set in New Baskerville: 11-1/2 pt on 17
Typesetting: Julie Cochrane
Printing: Hignell Printing, Winnipeg, Manitoba
Cover Design: Cecilia Jang
Cover Photo: John Yanyshyn, Visions West

The paper used in this book is Miami Vellum. It is recycled stock containing no dioxins. It is totally chlorine-free (TCF) as well as acid-free (therefore of archival quality). The paper is made from at least 10% post-consumer waste.

The publisher wishes to thank the Canada Council and the British Columbia Cultural Services Branch for their generous financial assistance.

CANADIAN CATALOGUING IN PUBLICATION DATA
Wilson, Gordon (Gordon F. D.), 1949–
  A civilized revolution

  ISBN 0-921870-40-X

  1. British Columbia—Politics and government—1991–
2. Progressive Democratic Alliance (B.C.)   I. Title.
FC3829.2.W54 1996   971.1'04   C96-910256-9
F1088.W54 1996

CONTENTS

TIME FOR A NEW ENGINE: CHANGING THE STRUCTURE OF GOVERNMENT

PAYING THE PRICE: WELFARE, EDUCATION, AND HEALTH CARE

SURVIVING CONFEDERATION: A BACKUP PLAN FOR BRITISH COLUMBIA   82

PREFACE

Politics is about power, and money buys power, hence politics is about money. Our governments, however, are about democracy which should, in a free society, supercede money. The strength of a democracy lies with its people's ability to make informed choices about those in whom they place their trust through the election process. In the final analysis, then, democracy is about people. We need leadership in our province and in our country which is focused on our people, that holds as its first priority investing in our people.

This book presents the Progressive Democratic Alliance's *blueprint* for change: its *challenge* to many of the assumptions on which our current political and economic institutions are based, and its plan for a *Civilized Revolution* in British Columbia. Those whose short-term economic success is dependent on government grants, programs, and policies that are contrary to the long-term interests of the majority of our people may find our program disconcerting. The average British Columbian, however, I am convinced will appreciate this attempt to provide a clear explanation of the steps we must take if we, our children and grandchildren, are to survive the 21st century.

Unfortunately, in many parliamentary democracies,

including our own in British Columbia, the real needs of the electorate are too often pushed aside by a seemingly endless crush of corporations, unions, and other vested interests in continuous line and competition for special government attention and an undeserved share of its $18 billion-plus annual budget—a situation that will continue so long as our politics and government centre on political parties which require large amounts of money for elections, or for otherwise advancing their agendas. He who pays the piper always calls the tune.

I think it important to emphasize that my decision to join the provincial Liberal Party in 1985 did not come out of a desire to become Premier, or Prime Minister, but rather out of a sense of frustration with the polarization of BC politics between the NDP and Social Credit, a polarization that denied the voters any measure of reasonable choice. My initial ambition was simply to breathe life into a provincial party that had been largely moribund for a decade. I doubt that many believed this situation would change when I was acclaimed its leader in 1987. Certainly, nobody that I know of coveted my job. Indeed, when the provincial election was called in 1991, Liberal party prospects did not seem remarkably better than they had in 1986, when we again failed to elect any of our candidates. We stood at a mere 6% in the polls. One televised leaders' debate, however, changed all that. Four weeks later, my party won 17 seats and 33% of the popular vote.

Even I was surprised at the magnitude of our success. How challenging my new role seemed that election evening, how unlikely just hours before that I would be Leader of the Official Opposition for the province of British Columbia! Certainly, I had known that my four years of work would pay dividends, but this far exceeded my expectations. I will always remember the air of anticipation as the invited guests, all dressed in their finest, entered the plush Chamber of the British Columbia Legislative Assembly to witness the swearing in of the MLAs elected to the Liberal Opposition. This was an historic occasion. It had been more than ten years since the last Liberal had sat in the House, and over forty years since the party held such prominence.

As unlikely a group as one could ever imagine, we stood in three rows on the plush red carpet before the Clerk's table in the centre of that beautiful carved-oak and marble-pillared chamber, each waiting his turn to be formally sworn in. As I heard the Legislative Clerk, Ian Horne, call my name, I can recall feeling both honoured and apprehensive: honoured to be given the trust of the electorate to represent them as the Leader of the Opposition; apprehensive because I also knew that over the previous four years, I had offended more than my share of closet Social Crediters within my own party.

For that moment, however, I could feel only a great pride in being part of the government of this great province. When I stepped forward to sign the register, I saw my mother and father seated nearby watching. I wondered what they were thinking. My son Mathew and my daughter Christina also looked on, their eyes sparkling, reflecting the lights that illuminated the Chamber from the decoratively painted ceiling above. This was for me the beginning of a new chapter in an already interesting life, and I could feel my family's pride as I took the oath of office, and signed my name in the official register: Gordon Frederick David Wilson, MLA, Leader of Her Majesty's Loyal Opposition.

In retrospect, signs of the storm that was gathering around my leadership were even then evident, if only in small, black clouds on the political horizon. Like any good sailor, I took time to check the charts, to right the compass, and to put to the wind only enough sheet to stay our heading. Had enough of my legislative and party crew remained loyal and not joined the Howe Street buccaneers who quickly boarded us from their sinking Socred ship, we might have repelled them to stay our small "l" liberal course. Instead, they surrendered almost en masse, exposing me to the barrage of undeserved contempt, personal ridicule, and public abuse that ultimately cost me my hard-earned 1991 position.

I am convinced it was my commitment to institutional and economic reform and the threat this posed to the established power elites in British Columbia that created the demand that I be removed from the leadership of the Liberal Party, and thus from the office of Leader of the Official Opposition of British Columbia. In the fall of 1993, I lost the leadership of the Liberal Party of BC to Gordon Campbell, then Mayor of Vancouver—another instant-Liberal—through a questionable "televote" convention process. And the province quickly regressed to its tradition of polarized politics.

I recall Dave Barrett, the former NDP Premier of British Columbia, coming over to my table in the parliamentary restaurant in Victoria in March or April 1994. He said, "I think what those b—ds did to you was despicable, but you had to see it coming. I could have told you that the Howe Street boys don't like anyone who doesn't play by their rules." If those were not his exact words, that was their purport.

Fortunately, those who so quickly turned against me could not take away my right to sit as a freely elected Member of the Legislative Assembly, nor could they remove the moral authority given my political leadership by 33% of British Columbia's voters. Initially, my senior political lieutenant, Judi Tyabji, and I left the Liberal party and its legislative caucus to sit as Independent Members of the Legislative Assembly. In December 1993, in order to provide a new political vehicle for those who wanted to protect our mandate to fight for change, we took on the challenge of starting again from the beginning, and became British Columbia's first Progressive Democratic Alliance MLAs.

It's tempting to enter into a long discussion of what transpired within the BC Liberal Party between my acclamation as its leader in 1987 and the coup that deposed me in 1993, but those events are already well chronicled by my colleague, and now my best friend and wife, Judi Tyabji. I strongly recommend her book, *Political Affairs*, because it provides rare insight into many recent events in the politics of our volatile province. And contrary to the rather superficial treatment it received in reviews and news articles by some members of the media, it is both well researched and entertaining.

As for the role of the media, especially television, in the

events that have most affected my life and career over these last few years, I had initially thought to dedicate a chapter in this book to exposing some of their shabby practices, and to set my personal record straight. On consideration, however, I think it pointless to feed further the indecent tastes of those few who believe a front page headline or top-billed story should dictate their ethics. Tales of past domestic disharmonies and turmoil within the Wilson family are old news, and of little value to anyone, least of all to my ex-wife, our two children (who have chosen to live with Judi and me), and Judi's three children who now complete our beautiful new family. Besides, the truth has always been there for those who would seek it.

To the extent that I have been successful in politics, I owe everything to the people of this province who want the sort of balanced responsible government that I promised to promote when I was elected as the Leader of the Opposition in 1991. And it is for them that I have written this book outlining in greater detail than ever before the PDA's course toward a civilized revolution: a new system of governance that will look to the individual needs of our citizens, fairly weighing those needs against the demands made by society as a whole. It was my commitment to this revolution that led me into politics in the first place. Politics should not be about political parties, their leaders, or their friends. It should be about the ordinary British Columbian: you, your family, your community, your province, and your country.

Progressive Democratic Alliance: the name tells it all. The PDA is made up of British Columbians who are *Progressive* in their outlook and policy, *Democratic* in their principles and procedures, in *Alliance* to serve the people, not the special/insider interest groups.

Gordon Wilson
Powell River, British Columbia
17 March 1996

BIOGRAPHICAL INTRODUCTION
BY JOHN MUNRO

It is said that one can gain some insight into the character of an individual by his or her heroes. If that is so, then make what you will of mine! Jesus Christ, who I believe was the world's most successful revolutionary figure, would top my list. Within modern history, however, Mahatma Gandhi, Martin Luther King, and Pierre Elliot Trudeau are individuals for whom I have the greatest admiration. What these men held in common was their commitment to justice, and to the rights and freedoms of the individual. All preached that with those rights comes responsibility. And each recognized the very fine line between the protection and benevolence of the state, and state-sponsored tyranny and persecution.

— Gordon Wilson

The philosophy Gordon Wilson subscribes to, the convictions he holds, and the political leadership he continues to offer British Columbians are, as with every individual, the products of character and circumstance—of inheritance uniquely shaped by everything encountered on the road of life. Thus, it is important that the reader be provided with at least some understanding of his background and, most particularly, of the people and events that have influenced significantly his perception of the world in which we live.

Gordon Wilson is a fifth generation Canadian, and third generation British Columbian, of Scottish descent on his father's side. The Wilsons are a sept of the clan Gunn, in which memories of past injustices and betrayals run deep. Gordon's grandfather was a hard-living, West Coast commercial fisherman; his paternal grandmother, a working class homemaker with a penchant for the ponies at Exhibition Park. Gordon's grandparents, however, believed in the value of education. Gordon's father (also named Gordon, as was his father and grandfather before him), not only graduated from the University of British Columbia, but went on to complete his PhD in anthropology at the University of London before establishing himself in the commercial life of East Africa.

Gordon's mother, Evelyn (neé Gilbert), is of Welsh descent, with a long family history that includes among its notables the half-brother of Sir Walter Raleigh, Sir Humphrey Gilbert, who established England's first North American colony at St. John's, Newfoundland, in 1583. According to family legend, however, a more direct relative was a pirate named Gilbert, who was allegedly renowned for his exploits against the Spanish treasure galleons.

Gordon's parents met at King Edward High School in Vancouver, when running against each other for the office of student president. Obviously, they survived each other's competitive natures. Their third child, and only son, was born several years later at the Vancouver General Hospital on 2 January 1949. When Gordon was little more than nine months old, his parents took him, and his sisters, Heather and Susan, to live in London, England, where his father was studying on a Lord Beaverbrook scholarship. From there they moved to Tanganyika (Tanzania), so that his father could complete his doctoral field work on the Barabaig people in a tiny, uncharted village called Katesh. Except for a year spent at school in BC's Okanagan Valley during the most violent period of the Mau Mau march to independence in Kenya, where the Wilson family finally settled, Gordon would live in East Africa until 1965.

One doesn't have to talk long with Gordon Wilson to appreciate that his African childhood had an indelible influence on his thinking. He claims that witnessing first-hand many of the native African peoples' struggles for freedom taught him the danger of taking individual liberties for granted. And although he probably couldn't give a political speech today in the Ki-Swahili he learned as a toddler, there seems little question that his youthful experiences also provided him with a profound respect for the diversity of human cultures and traditions.

As a particular illustration of what he has in mind, he tells a story set at his Kenyan home in the late 1950s, when the Mau Mau, a secret society within the Kikuyu tribe, became a significant threat to the peace and well-being of many Africans, as well as the handful of Europeans who lived on the rural farmlands and within the forests that skirt the capital city of Nairobi. Recalling the nightly drum beats that still echo in his mind, he says that fear was palpable amongst the people, whether black or white. Fear of arbitrary arrest by the colonial police and the British military on the one hand, and fear for one's life at the hands of the Mau Mau on the other. (Wilson, of course, is quick to point out that he later came to understand that the Mau Mau was largely an independence movement, albeit tribal in nature, and that few non-African people were ever directly threatened.) In the event, however, he was awakened one morning by loud noises outside his bedroom window. He pulled back his curtain to find the police, with rifles at the ready, rounding up the several Africans who were employed by his parents, including the family's gardener (and father of his two playmates), who was being dragged out of the small house in which he lived, half clothed, arms wrenched behind his back, hands in cuffs. Although Gordon's mother, who was at the time a senior civil servant in the Kenyan Ministry of Community Development, was later able to intervene to secure their release, Wilson says that he will always remember the look of terror in the eyes of his little friends, and the cries of their mother, as their father was hauled away at the point of a gun. That the state can trample the rights of innocent individuals in the name of peace and security—in this case, simply because they couldn't tell one Kikuyu from another—was, he reflects, a powerful lesson for an eight-year-old boy to learn. And a lesson not to be forgotten these forty years later, when the Canadian public is calling out for greater enforcement powers for our police.

A second incident that remains clearly stamped in Wilson's memory was the visit he made when barely into his teens to a Frente de Libertação de Moçambique (Frelimo) rebel camp within the southern borders of what was then Tanganyika. (Frelimo was a guerrilla organization dedicated to the independence of the Portuguese colony of Mozambique.) His visit there was made possible because of the friendship that his parents had with Eduardo Mondlane, an academic with an American wife, who was the leader of the rebel forces. One evening over dinner at the Wilson home outside Nairobi, Mondlane thought to cure the young Wilson's naive impressions about the nature of war by suggesting Gordon travel during his next school break to Dar es Salaam, where the senior Wilson had a company branch office, and travel with him to the Frelimo camp. Gordon did so, and was appalled to discover first hand what war really meant: dismembered, blinded, burned, and brutalized children, women, and men, the true victims of armed conflict. Nowhere to be seen were the popular press images of smiling men in fatigues, waving their rifles while riding high on tanks and armoured cars. Eduardo Mondlane was killed less than a year later in his Dar es Salaam headquarters by a bomb that had been placed under his chair by someone close within his ranks.

At the age of sixteen years in 1965, armed with his university entrance, the obviously precocious young Wilson bussed and hitchhiked through the Middle East and Europe, arriving finally in Dublin, where he bought an airline ticket to New York and a Greyhound Bus 99-day tour of America. Arriving at Kennedy International Airport, he plunged headlong into American society. It was nothing short of culture shock. Without going into the details of his 36-state tour, or his several detours into Canada, his education into the realities of the "great American way" was swift, and sometimes brutal. This was not at all the America of the *National Geographic!*

As he recalls, he found it difficult to reconcile the burned-out houses of the black neighbourhoods of Chicago with the glass towers of corporate America in the downtown core. How was it possible, he asked himself, that the United States, which so prided itself as the first and finest among nations, could allow the sores of injustice to fester so openly. Perhaps he found part of the answer in the streets of Little Rock, Arkansas, when he came to the aid of a small black boy who had been viciously kicked out of the way by two "good old boys" who were in the process of repossessing the family furniture. He also learned that it required up-front cash to suture the wounds he received in a severe beating for his "nigger-lovin" ways!

It was, of course, experiences such as these that made all the more poignant the now immortal "I have a dream" speech of Martin Luther King, Jr. for the privileged white colonial boy who joined the multitudes one steamy August afternoon in Washington, D.C., to hear that remarkable black leader articulate a vision of equality among all people, of all colours. King, a man who shunned the trappings of elected office, moved tens of thousands of souls that day— including Gordon Wilson's.

At summer's end, Gordon entered the State University College at New Paltz, a small town on the Wallkill River, in

Ulster County in southeastern New York, where he earned an Honours BSc in geography under the distinguished direction of Professor Robert Knapp in just three years. Indeed, Wilson so excelled in his courses that he was awarded a scholarship enabling him to spend most of his final year in Japan working on a comparative land-use study in the southern portion of the main Island of Honshu, in a relatively small community called Shimizu. It was there that he met a Buddhist priest who invited him to stay at his monastery. Ever curious about cultures and religions different from his own, Gordon did so, and discovered a new definition of freedom in the humility and sanctified poverty of the priests, something he thinks worth remembering in a western world so driven by hubris, greed, and overconsumption.

At this juncture, the reader will be forgiven for thinking that this biographical sketch has been cribbed from an early edition of *Boys' Own Annual,* and that the next stage of Gordon Wilson's youthful adventures would take him to Xanadu. The problem, so far as there is one, is that the picture perforce is unbalanced by a brevity that does not allow for memories of childhood high jinks, sibling rivalries, family holidays, best friends, favourite teachers, O-level exams, university student politics, weekend beer parties, or even travelling to Woodstock in a beat-up Valiant to hear the legends of American rock. Instead, we are confined to plumbing the largely exotic circumstances that shaped his early sense of political mission and the breadth of his young vision.

At the age of twenty, his American undergraduate

degree in hand, Gordon Wilson returned to Vancouver, the city of his birth, to do graduate studies in political and economic geography at the University of British Columbia. It was during these years that he met Elizabeth Kool, whom he married in 1972 (without benefit of media attention), when he was twenty-three and she was seventeen. Their two children Christina and Mathew were born in 1975 and 1976 respectively.

Of course, in 1972, neither Gordon nor his young bride had any thought that their union might be less than either expected it to be. The future, naturally, lay at their feet. And when a job offer came to Gordon from Capilano College to teach geography to first- and second-year students, he put on hold his plans to add a University of Alberta PhD to his UBC Masters degree. Instead, they worked to put together a down payment on a small house in Burnaby—something still possible for newlyweds in the early 1970s. In 1977, they traded this for acreage on the Sunshine Coast, built a commodious log house in which to raise their family, and developed a small but productive hog farm.

In the eight years that passed between their idealistic decision to embrace the simpler life and Gordon's entry into provincial politics, Gordon continued to teach at Capilano College, where he was elected to a term as president of his faculty association, and twice acted as the chief negotiator in their contract negotiations. In his home community, he developed an interest in amateur theatre, wrote several plays that were produced locally and around the province, and served on the executive of the North Shore zone of Theatre

BC. And somewhere in between, he found time to coach his son's soccer team, and build a stable for his daughter's horses.

His first foray into politics came with his election to the Sunshine Coast Regional District Board in 1985, a position that he held until his election to provincial office in 1991. Local government, Wilson contends, represents democracy's "front lines", because it provides opportunity to serve one's community in a very direct way. He lists the school of music at Pender Harbour, Katherin Lake park, expanded community golf facilities, and the preservation of government wharves for commercial and sports fishers alike, as among the things he helped to achieve.

Obviously, the critical moment in Wilson's life came when he accepted the leadership of the Liberal Party of British Columbia in 1987. Building a political organization virtually from scratch, with precious little initial help, and even less money, is no easy task. It begins by taking a leave-of-absence from your job to spend your own money travelling the length and breadth of the province for weeks on end, seeking out prospective candidates and volunteers in each of the 75 constituencies. It involves countless hours developing appropriate reform policies, writing and sending out hundreds of press releases, making speech after service-club speech, and talking to every reporter, editor, and hot-line host who will give you his or her time. And most often it involves a personal cost in terms of quality family-time that mere dollars cannot cover.

Politics, as some American wit once observed, makes

for estranged bedfellows. Somewhere along the way, possibly even before his foray into local government, Gordon and Elizabeth Wilson began to develop their individual potentials in mutually exclusive ways—hardly an uncommon occurrence at any level in our society, especially among those who marry at a early age. There is no doubt, however, that what God had joined together, politics finally rent asunder. Elizabeth Wilson asked her husband for a divorce on the eve of the televised leaders' debate during the 1991 provincial election.

Fate, karma, call it what you will: had the Wilson marriage ended in divorce at any time before it did (as well it might have), its failure would never have become part of a national news story. Perhaps, then, the working press would have found less sport in Gordon's mature romance and subsequent successful marriage and political partnership with Judi Tyabji. Although I think not. In today's world, public men and women are only allowed private lives if they are incredibly dull, and Gordon's and Judi's were anything but.

Of course, Gordon Wilson can be faulted for being blind to these realities. He was no longer in academe, where private matters, however complex, hardy raise an eyebrow. He is, however, probably correct when he suggests that had he played "the game" demanded by the right-wing movers and shakers who joined the Liberal party after the 1991 election, several major media outlets would have put a lid on their coverage.

He can also be faulted for not realizing his extreme political vulnerability. A Liberal party with a very small membership base, under his leadership, had won an electoral prize that confounded the predictions of every psephologist in the province. More than the New Democrats under Mike Harcourt, who were about to form the government, the Wilson Liberals had destroyed forever the discredited Bill Vander Zalm/Rita Johnston Social Credit Party. British Columbia's establishment power brokers, who'd enjoyed nearly forty years of comfort in the anti-socialist coalition that the Bennetts, father and son, had built, now determined they had little choice but to make the new Official Opposition their own—with or without Gordon Wilson at its head. That decision made, two-thirds of those formerly associated with Social Credit (by popular estimate, at least) began to shift their allegiance to the provincial Liberals.

If only Wilson had been more accommodating. If only he had agreed to do no more than pay lip-service to his reform platform and had instead, like Mackenzie King after the federal Liberal convention of 1919, championed established vested interests; if only he had not been the only prominent BC politician to campaign against the Charlottetown Accord; if only he had been amenable to all the secret deals that are life-blood to the apparatchiks who now surrounded him: if only he had been a *typical* politician! Then, he might have survived as leader of the BC Liberals, and escaped much of the obloquy engendered in the media by his domestic situation. To his credit, and as the pages of this book clearly demonstrate, there is nothing typical about Gordon Wilson.

Both Gordon Wilson and Judi Tyabji have more than

paid the price of their idealism and humanity. What is more, they have established reputations, even among their harshest critics, as being among the hardest working and most effective MLAs this province has ever seen. And Gordon is judged by many of his peers to be the best debater in today's Legislative Assembly. Thus far, they appear to have given their electors more than full value. They believe they have more to offer. To this end, Gordon has put pen to paper to detail in the pages that follow the platform of his Progressive Democratic Alliance party.

*   *   *

The above "Introduction" is no more than it pretends to be: a brief biographical sketch of a unique political personality. Most of the information contained therein was, of course, provided by my subject, but I accept responsibility for its final selection and shape and for such editorial comment as I have chosen to make. I belong to no provincial political party. My tasks as Gordon Wilson's editor have been purely professional. Still, I think it fair to say that I have enjoyed my brief association with Mr. Wilson, and the opportunity this has provided me to reconsider many of the political and economic issues that affect the province in which I live.

John Munro
Vancouver, British Columbia
21 March 1996

LIMITS TO GROWTH:

OUR FUNDAMENTAL RESOURCE BASE

Most readers will remember the heart-rending, television appeals of a few years ago to help feed the starving multitudes in northeastern Africa. Unfortunately, legitimate media coverage of this human tragedy made little of the fact that in 1900 over 40% of the geographical region in question was forested, whereas by 1990 less than four percent had forest cover. Or that the untrammelled exploitation of what had proved a quick-cash crop had depleted the once-rich land and left desert in its place. Indeed, only a few news reports exposed the direct relationship between resource depletion and the resultant, indelible images of absolute and shocking destitution.

You probably didn't hear this on the evening news either, but a recent United Nations report estimated that the world's forests would be reduced by an area the size of 40 Californias during the last two decades of this century. Of course, here at home in British Columbia, we have made our own substantial contribution to this approaching global catastrophe. When BC's forest companies moved their huge clear-cutting operations from the valley bottoms and gentle hills to the steep slopes and hanging valleys of our mountain ranges, the result was massive soil erosion. And once eroded, those soils became nutrient deficient or simply non-existent, leaving us an inheritance of barren land. Much of the regulation and legislation that now protects the richness of our forests' soils was enacted only after decades of such practices had resulted in great and irreparable damage.

Throughout the world an estimated 25 billion tons of arable top soil are lost every year. Indeed, it is projected by the US National Research Council that, by the year 2000, deserts will have expanded globally by an area one and one-half times the size of the United States. The implications of this for future food production and human sustainability are staggering. Where nations once fought for control of the world's supplies of gold, silver, silks, and spices, tomorrow's struggle will be for food.

It is perhaps most ironic that of all the things Canadians take for granted, food tops the list. Sure, we might protest when we have to pay a bit more for what we buy, and sometimes there is a run on coffee or sugar when climatic conditions or international events threaten supply, but few Canadians know that since 1986, when world grain reserves were sufficient to feed the world for 101 days, consumption has outpaced production to the extent that today's reserves are at a record low. According to the World Watch Institute, carry-over stocks have declined for the third year in a row, and are at an estimated 49-day supply—"just enough to ensure supply between farmers and urban consumers". Because food scarcity has never been a critical issue in Canada, Canadians are generally unaware of the coming global fight for food. Nor have we considered the continued decline of our domestic agricultural industry in this context.

GLOBAL POPULATION

In 1830, the earth's human population passed the one billion mark. A hundred years later, it passed the two billion mark. A mere thirty years after that, in 1960, global population passed the three billion mark. And by 1975, our numbers had surpassed 4 billion. Twenty years later, in 1995, our numbers stood at over six billion. And in thirty years more, our human population will reach an incomprehensible twelve billion people!

Within the lifetime of our own so-called Generation X, three *billion* young people, virtually all of them residing in what is commonly referred to as the developing world, will reach their reproductive years. These potential parents are not conjectured; they are alive today. This is a generation that I call *Generation R.* Just what this R becomes known for depends largely on the action or inaction of today's politicians within the developed world. Certainly, they will be Generation *Reproduction,* but, depending on today's leader-

3

ship, they will be either Generation *Reform,* or Generation *Revolution* as well.

In the past, western political interests have always been content to point an accusing finger at the developing world, where 90% of the global population increase occurs, "tsk tsk-ing" that the city planners of Calcutta have to build the equivalent in size of a present-day Vancouver every year. What we have failed to grasp is that these once-sedentary populations are now highly mobile, and that the only barriers to their international movement are those put there by immigration regulations of potential host countries.

And given the distribution of world resources, wealth, and human population, it is clear that we are on the verge of the next major global migration. When this movement starts in earnest, human populations will move across the oceans like a huge tidal wave, and no amount of regulation will keep out those who seek survival in one of the last remaining areas of liveable space with potable water: Canada.

THE NEW ECONOMIC PARADIGM

A growing number of British Columbians today are looking for a scapegoat, some individual or group to blame for whatever it is that ails them socially and economically. They have become cynical about their politicians and the institutions that govern them. The status quo, whether in religion, education, politics, or our social order as a whole, is being challenged daily. Regrettably, not all of these challenges to conventional authority are positive. There is a growing intolerance of those on income assistance, and a rising tide of resentment against immigrants, especially those of different colour.

Social backlash, however, will never provide us the new economic paradigm our future demands. We need instead to challenge some of capitalism's basic principles. The prevailing corporate wisdom is that British Columbian interests are best served by the preservation of an economy based on a strong resource sector. Such thinking fails even to acknowledge that our resource base, which once provided an almost unlimited harvest in trees, fish, minerals, and water, is fast becoming depleted. It is the reality of this depletion, and its ultimate consequences, that have created the need to abandon outdated economic theories.

SUSTAINABILITY

Since 1987, it has been fashionable to embrace the Brundtland Commission concept of "Sustainable Development". The thesis of the Brundtland Report, *Our Common Future,* was that our current economic practices (i.e., growth) were sustainable, although a more equitable distribution of wealth and product among the world's population was desirable. "Sustainable Development" thus became the rallying cry for all those who held a stake in the economic status quo because it provided them a respectable rationalization for continuing virtually unrestricted exploitation of our natural resource base. It was even used by developers, posing as environmentalists, to carry on business as usual.

As a resource economist, I took issue with the concept of Sustainable Development from the outset. And it comes as no surprise to me that today there are many who challenge its premise, and agree that this concept is fundamentally flawed. As noted above, our population is expanding exponentially, and will double within the next thirty years. With that growth will come increased expectations for resource consumption that cannot be met.

In response to the increasing rejection of the concept of Sustainable Development by experts in the field, those involved in the planning of our economy, especially those in its resource sector, have dropped the notion of growth from their jargon in favour of "Sustainability". However, they seem to assume that Sustainability means no less than maintaining the status quo in terms of levels of consumption, something I maintain cannot be achieved without widening the gap between the rich and poor, and without further erosion of our environmental base.

Clearly, the solution to our economic crisis lies in accepting that there are real and very firm *limits to growth*. We need to change the manner by which we measure the economic effect of our actions, and in doing so, institute procedures that protect our environment. Indeed, I have long believed that the most successful politician will be the one who recognizes that, notwithstanding our general adherence to western capitalist economics, our human survival rests with our ability to live within a strategy of *limits to growth*.

THE LIMITS TO GROWTH

Limits to growth is not a new concept. One of The Club of Rome reports in the late 1960s raised the critical issue of the dramatic rise in global population, and the consequent need to examine carefully the physical limits of our global environment. Now, nearly a generation later, only the most irresponsible among us would suggest a long-term economic policy that is premised on either "sustainable development" or "sustainability". As a result, planning for the new global village must be focused solely on *limits to growth*.

Limits to growth means exactly what it says: that there are very real, finite limits to the growth of human populations and their consumption of the world's resources. Beyond these finite limits, the world's ecosystems can no longer sustain life in any recognizable form. Unfortunately, there are no clearly visible lines, with accompanying signs that read, "DO NOT CROSS", to mark these limits. Rather, there are physical thresholds, as evidenced by our obviously thinning ozone layer, which when exceeded will challenge our ability to survive as a species. However much we may have benefited in the past from western capitalist economics, we must all recognize that our human salvation is dependent upon our ability to live within *limits to growth*.

THINKING GLOBALLY

British Columbians must recognize the plight of the one billion people in our world who live in absolute poverty. It is important for us to understand the needs of the three billion people who have inadequate sanitation, the one and one-half billion who have no health care, and the one billion seven hundred thousand who don't have a safe source of water. We must face the fact that one child in three on our planet is seriously malnourished. We must accept our responsibility to do something for these children, and work to eliminate their deprivation.

The relative wealth of present-day British Columbians cannot long isolate them from global reality. We are but a small part of the new global village, and as such we have a duty to our dispossessed neighbours. We cannot ignore their cries. Why then do we have little or no debate within the BC Legislature over such matters? Why is it that when these matters are raised by the Progressive Democratic Alliance MLAs, voices on both the right and the left urge us to tend only to the business of the people of BC? A major reason is that many MLAs are elected through the munificence of established economic interests that will be directly threatened by such debate. Unfortunately, the interests of all British Columbians will be threatened if we do not acknowledge the larger, global issues, and prepare for them locally.

THE NEW GLOBAL VILLAGE

The 1980s and '90s brought a communications revolution, with cellular telephones and instant access to the world through the Internet, which completed the reduction of our once formidable world to a global village—a development first anticipated by Canadian communications guru, Marshall McLuhan, in his 1968 book with Quentin Fiore, *War and Peace in the Global Village.* In the next century, however, we will be challenged by the need to develop new ways to live together, as the world's resource base becomes smaller, and the demands of an exploding population become greater. *A New Social Contract for the New Global Village* will have to be devised and effected, if we are to endure economically, with our individual freedoms and dignity intact.

The breakdown of our present social contract can be traced to those major corporations which have acquired unaccountable power through their domination of our economy. These companies, whose only raison d'être is the maximization of profits at whatever cost to the societies in which they operate, are not only the very antithesis of democratic, decision-making institutions, their instant financial mobility places them beyond the control of most governments.

The price of democracy, however, is eternal vigilance. And to survive, we, in British Columbia, will be forced finally to re-think the structure of our government, our system of justice, the distribution of wealth between rich and poor, how we provide education, health care, and social services, our views on urbanization, land management and tenure. Most of all, we will have to re-think established economic theories.

What we need in British Columbia is an approach to the management of our natural resources that keeps wealth within our province by directing the bounty of our forests, farms, mines, and ocean to local mills, processors, and value-added industries. Only when we take a serious approach to the needs of local operators will we stop the erosion of our primary resource base, and achieve our economic potential. This approach must be coupled with a production strategy that encompasses not simply the immediate use of our manufactures, but also their end use. Reusing and recycling must become an integral part of the production process.

Similarly, we will have to introduce standards to measure adequately the real cost of production, which must include the cost to the environment at every stage, from production to consumption to waste-disposal, including the possible restoration of the environment. In that the international community currently holds no such standards of responsibility, we will be at an economic disadvantage to those jurisdictions that are prepared to destroy the environment in pursuit of short-term profit. Consequently, a commitment to such a process will be difficult to maintain until global competition is forced into line by enlightened self-interest—which is why the years ahead will require leadership with a vision for a more just society, where a better balance exists between humankind and our ecosystem.

THE HYDROSPHERE

There was never much argument, when breathable air was still taken for granted, that, of our three fundamental resources—air, land, and water—water, or more broadly stated, the hydrosphere, is the most critical to our survival.

Without potable water, human life cannot exist. This, at least, is something that we all seem to understand. Certainly, British Columbians are quick to become exercised over anything that threatens their potable water supplies. Indeed, there is a growing number of people who will take to the streets, block roads, even go to jail to prevent such things as logging in our watersheds. And they quite rightly demand that their water resources receive full protection under the law—whether the jurisdiction concerned is municipal, provincial, federal, or international.

The difficulty for those who make government policy, however, is that water can be contaminated in many ways. Consequently, even when protected in its physical form, water cannot be eliminated from the equation that balances the cost of each growth opportunity. We must recognize that land-use policy will impact on ground water supply and quality, and that everything we put into the air will in some way get into our water.

THE ATMOSPHERE

To its credit, the NDP government under Mike Harcourt started to introduce clean-air legislation, largely based upon the example set in California. There are, of course, those who argue that the polluters in the developing countries are doing far more damage than we are, and that because we share the same atmosphere, the best legislation in British Columbia will not prevent pollution drifting in from afar, and will only serve to reduce our competitive advantage by increasing the cost of production and scaring away potential investors.

While there is always some truth in objections of this sort, the fact is that it is only through a vigorous adherence to strict anti-pollution regulations in the democracies of the developed world that we will be able to insist on an equal standard in the developing world. After all, there really is no such thing as a first world, second world, or third world. There is but one world, and it belongs to six billion individuals.

Besides, it is not the people of the developing countries who thrive on industries that pollute but the corporations who profit. Now ask yourself where the controlling interests in those corporations reside. For the most part, they live within the upper-class settlements of the developed countries, where they and their families are free from the very pollution that provides them the means to live as they do. So where should the global-class-action law suits start? At the top.

There is no doubt that British Columbia needs a Clean Air Act that prohibits the discharge of fluorocarbons, excesses of carbon dioxide and other noxious gases that alter the balance within the atmosphere. Clearly, one of the most pressing global concerns today is the depletion of the ozone layer, which results in unfiltered ultraviolet light reaching the surface of the earth. Although the net impact of this is not fully understood, we do know that higher incidences of skin cancer have resulted, and that crops are often damaged as well.

Of even greater significance, however, is the potentially disastrous impact of unfiltered ultraviolet light on the largest producer of oxygen on the planet: the phytoplankton, microscopic organisms that float and drift in the upper layers of our oceans, lakes, and the still waters of our rivers and streams. We hear so often about the clearcutting of the Amazon jungles, which is correctly tied to the reduction of the earth's oxygen supply. But any large decline in phytoplankton would be far more serious—akin, if you like, to a massive infection of the lungs in a human being.

THE LITHOSPHERE, OUR LAND

The demand on any land base is driven by significant increases in population. In the province of British Columbia, with a population of little more than three million, few would suggest there is an immediate problem. But this is not necessarily so. Our population problem exists in the distribution of people, not their numbers. Further, the lack of planning to accommodate future increases in our population is certain to exacerbate this problem. BC politicians should be engaged in a Sixty Year Plan that anticipates our eventual growth from three to over ten million people.

Regrettably, the majority among us who own land regard it as a commodity. As such, its productive value is a distant second to its market value, which may translate into huge profits for those who hold its tenure when demand is greater than supply. We need to re-think our values.

Our use of the land will have to change dramatically

over the next generation. Even if global population is limited to a zero growth rate, internal migration of people from eastern Canada, northern movement from the United States, and even limited immigration from overseas will combine to bring about the increase in BC's population that is forecast above. I may not be here to witness this, but if I were, I might well thank those politicians who had the foresight to plan such growth without alienating the foreshore, the lakeshore, our watersheds, and the commons within our water corridors.

The Progressive Democratic Alliance, while recognizing the fundamental right of citizens to acquire and own their land fee simple, challenges the notion that any individual should have absolute freedom to use his or her land in a manner that detracts from the environmental integrity of the surrounding property. In other words, the right to own land must be protected, but within the realm of a defined common interest. A recent debate on the right of an individual in the interior to clear-cut private land is a case in point. While clear cutting may be good for the landowner's pocket book, removing timber in that fashion can have a devastating effect on surrounding property because of surface runoff, soil erosion, flash flooding, rock and mud slides, and often a profound change to wildlife habitat.

The *Limits to Growth* Policy of the Progressive Democratic Alliance calls for proper management of our land base, and strict regulations to prevent the pollution of our water and air. To achieve this, our very first order of business will be to conduct a full and accurate inventory of all our resources so that we know what we have, and, more importantly, what we are likely to lose in any land-use decision. We will also attempt to foster a broad public recognition of the fact that it is time we took a different approach to our lifestyles, and moved away from an economy based upon carbon fuels toward more modern and cleaner energy sources such as electricity and hydrogen.

RESEARCH AND DEVELOPMENT

All of this will require a government that pays more than lip service to research and development opportunities within our institutes, universities, and the private sector. We need a government that will be aggressive in seeking solutions to environmental problems at their source. Under a Progressive Democratic Alliance government, post-secondary funding would be priorized to ensure that dedicated dollars are provided to our research institutions to develop new methods of dealing with the environmental consequences of our present economic activities, and to anticipate some of the challenges of the coming century and possible technological responses. There would also be tax incentives for entrepreneurs who *successfully* pursue such research and development through their own companies.

THE CORE INITIATIVE (1992-1995)

Soon after their election in 1991, BC's NDP government hired former Ombudsman Stephen Owen to head up the Commission on Resources and Environment (CORE), which was mandated to develop a provincial land-use strategy in consultation with economic and other stakeholders and members of the public at large. CORE was to draw up a parks plan to meet the Brundtland Commission's recommendation that 12% of the land base be set aside in protected areas. Although its basic concept was sound, CORE's terms of reference were deficient in two major respects. First, CORE was not mandated to conduct a comprehensive inventory of our resources; second, its decisions and resultant land-use policy were without prejudice to future Aboriginal land-settlements. Without a resource inventory, there was no way of knowing what the real impact of decisions taken to implement the province's land strategy would be on local and global economies and ecosystems. It was hard even to understand the criteria on which CORE's decisions were based.

To suggest that there is a desperate need in this province for a comprehensive land and resource inventory is to understate the case. How is it possible for the Aboriginal land claims resolution process or CORE to proceed sensibly without one? Should the Progressive Democratic Alliance form the government, it will move immediately to rectify this deficiency.

COMMUNITY INVOLVEMENT IN LAND-USE DECISIONS

The response of the people of the province to the CORE recommendations was to protest on the lawns of the legislature when the Vancouver Island plan was announced, to create a new coalition movement when the Cariboo/Interior plan was announced, and to become very vocal when the Kootenay plan was made public. In each of these cases, the Premier responded with a political compromise, arbitrarily altering the CORE findings in favour of considerations related more to the outcome of the next election than to the interests of the next generation.

Obviously, the other matter that needs to be addressed when considering the future of the CORE process is giving priority to the involvement of affected communities. When making decisions that have an impact on people's backyards, it is always advisable to speak to them first. Nine out of ten local problems have local solutions, and often a problem perceived from afar goes away when studied up close. These communities, then, require a greater voice or, at least, one that will be heard from the outset, in proceedings that are destined to affect them. Besides, they possess a base of local knowledge crucial to beginning the preparation of a provincial resource inventory.

FOOD STRATEGIES AND AGRICULTURE

Although only 8% of BC's land base is available for farming or cattle ranching, agriculture is a part of our economy that has not been given the time and attention it deserves. This is especially so because there is mounting evidence to suggest that California, the principal producer of our food today, will be subjected to a great deal of seismic activity in the next decade. This will cause significant change in its micro-climate and food production potential. Consequently, of all of the *Limits to Growth* issues that we face, the maintenance and protection of agriculture in British Columbia must be close to number one.

Because the Progressive Democratic Alliance is committed to the integrity of BC's agricultural land base, it recognizes that if we are to keep farmers on their land, there must be a reasonable opportunity for them to succeed economically. For the most part, Canada's agricultural programs have been steadily dismantled over the last decade, while property taxes have risen, and new regulations affecting employment practices, the restricted use of pesticides, etc., have increased farm costs. Because of the absence of any coherent food strategy in Canada, we, in BC, must make a renewed commitment to our farmers so that they can maximize food production, as well as to the food processing and canning industries that have experienced decline over the past generation.

Consequently, the very last thing we need is to elect politicians who are financed by individuals who have a special interest in directing land use away from agriculture. It has been said by editorial writers that the last thirty years of Social Credit gave us government run by used car salesmen always ready to "cut a deal". Beware, because the next wave of politicians may be developers quite ready to use their influence to advance their particular lists of private projects at the expense of our province's precious agricultural land base.

THE AGRICULTURAL LAND RESERVE

During the years 1972 to 1975, the NDP government in British Columbia introduced the Agricultural Land Reserve, or ALR, to prevent the sale of agricultural land for any purpose other than farming. Today, however, an increasing number of people are demanding that the ALR be scrapped, and that farmers be allowed to do with their land as they choose. The Land Owners Rights Association, or LORA, which purports to represent these disaffected interests, contends that it is unconstitutional to bind individuals to the land, and that they should be permitted to have their land rezoned for other uses. Obviously, there are huge profits to be made in the sale of farmland for development purposes.

On the one hand, farmers have a legitimate point of view. First of all, they own their land fee simple, as an investment which is now their old age security. Unlike salaried or union employees, most farmers do not enjoy pension, medical, dental, or other work-related benefits. The farmer has to depend upon his or her ability to make a decent living from the land, with little or no control over variable markets or packing and transportation costs. It is because at least some farmers benefit from the stability provided by supply management controls that the Progressive Democratic Alliance has committed itself to maintaining agricultural marketing boards. More must be done, however, if we are to overcome the desire of a significant number of BC farmers to destroy the ALR.

Canada, morever, is increasingly under attack for having agricultural subsidies that, according to our competitors to the south, provide our farmers with unfair advantages—a charge to which I say, "rubbish"! BC farmers face new challenges every year. Where they once benefited from Farm Income Insurance, a companion program to the ALR which was terminated in 1994, farmers now face undue hardship. Besides, as a sovereign country, we have every right to provide farmers an adequate financial package in recognition of the important role that they play in our economy. Consider the food shortages we all may face if, for lack of economic incentive, the next generation abandons the agricultural industry.

THE AGRICULTURAL LAND BANK SOLUTION

So, how do we best tackle this problem? First, we should recognize the value of the ALR. This is an asset to all British Columbians, the cost of which should be shared by the entire population. In other words, because a secure agricultural land base is in the best interests of the population as a whole, the population as a whole should pay for it.

To achieve this, the Progressive Democratic Alliance proposes to replace the ALR with an Agricultural Land Bank (ALB), into which each farmer would be permitted to deposit the title to his or her fee-simple land, and have this deposit recorded at a dollar figure determined by a fair-market, comparative-assessment process. The value of the land in question would be fixed by an independent government agency or sub-contractor. Owners who felt the value assigned their agricultural holdings was not an accurate reflection of the market would be given the opportunity to appeal any such decision to an appeals board struck for this purpose alone. Once the value of the land was determined, its owner would have the opportunity to collect annual interest on his or her deposit.

Although its title would not change, the land so deposited would be encumbered to the extent that the ALB would have the sole right to take a mortgage against it. Our agricultural land would then become part of the overall wealth of the province, and the capital on deposit would be fully secured by the government. In addition, a Farm Development Guarantee would be established to provide long-term, fully-secured, low-interest loans to provide farmers even greater security. In effect, we would be creating a partnership between the province and the agricultural land owner.

One difficulty in setting up the ALB would be including those farmlands already encumbered though conventional mortgages and loans. In these cases, the value on deposit would necessarily be diminished by the total amount outstanding, if those loans were to be paid out by the ALB. Because this would leave very little in terms of equity on deposit for many farmers, the province would have to undertake a one-time-only offer of support to farmers who wish to have the full value of their land on deposit, and carry by separate agreement an amortized payout of the original loans in their name. Thus we would eliminate forever the necessity of farmers having to contend with the hard-line borrowing policies of the chartered banks.

SHORT-TERM COST FOR LONG-TERM GAIN

Before the critics sharpen their pencils and attack this proposition, let me acknowledge that what I am proposing for BC's farmers is generous indeed. However, it is based upon the premise that our farm land and domestic agricultural industry is worth preserving, and that the cost related thereto should be carried by the population as a whole, and not simply by the farmer. It also provides the farmer an opportunity to "cash out" without removing land from the ALB by finding another investor who may wish to buy into his or her account. The simple fact is that if we fail to take some positive action to save and secure it, the family farm may soon cease to exist within our province.

Our plan to make farming in BC a profitable industry, I believe, will avoid challenge under the rather complex set of prohibitions set out in Canada's Free Trade Agreement with the United States, and reinforced by the North American Free Trade Agreement, which includes Mexico. It also should avoid the unfair trade claims that undoubtedly will be charged against Canada at the next round of the GATT negotiations.

PLANNING FOR GENERATION "R"

As mentioned earlier in this chapter, the rapid rise in global population with the advent of *Generation R* is not speculation. These people are alive today and have children at an early age. What is more, with the advances in medical technology, more of us will live longer to compound further our social, economic, and environmental problems.

Generation R will inherit the land as we leave it, complete with such developments that we (and previous generations) have allowed. If we have ruined our soils through chemical additions, if we have alienated our farmland by pavement and golf courses, if we have denuded our forests without thought to appropriate silviculture, then *Generation R* will have a very tough time, and they will hold us responsible. This may not be entirely fair, but we cannot shirk our responsibility by pointing to our parents and grandparents. It is up to us to fix whatever is wrong with our present land-use practices.

Further, if we are to succeed with our plan for balanced growth, we must overcome the biased view that *Limits to Growth* economics is a *negative* strategy that will result only in economic stagnation. Nothing could be further from the truth. In the next several decades, the greatest wealth-creating industries will be those that have as their primary function conserving drinkable water, feeding people nutritious food, managing waste through conversion and reduction, and working tirelessly to restore our natural environment with a proper land-use strategy and a more sensible design for the transportation and housing of people.

THE RESPONSIBILITY OF THE VOTERS

The obvious place to initiate a *Limits to Growth* strategy is with the politicians themselves when they next seek a mandate to form the government. The voters should withhold their votes from any politician representing any party that fails to provide a detailed, written plan for a *Limits to Growth* economic strategy. I only hope that it is not too late to put in place a democratic model for long-term planning and development.

TIME FOR A NEW ENGINE:

CHANGING THE STRUCTURE OF GOVERNMENT

If you own a 1965 Chevy with a 445 cubic inch, V8 automatic transmission, you don't expect to get a fuel efficiency equal to that of the newest, 1996 design in engines. No matter who drives the car, there is a physical limit to its fuel efficiency. To be sure, a careless driver with a heavy foot will burn more fuel per kilometre, but even the most careful driver will not be able to get the engine to perform beyond the maximum that its design allows.

The same is true of government. Because we make real demands on our politicians and have real expectations of government, we tend to drive that engine to its maximum level of performance without much regard for fuel efficiency. The results are massive annual deficits and greater long-term public debt. A change in the governing political party, like changing the driver of the '65 Chevy, will do little to change the overall fuel efficiency, because the engine itself no longer meets our needs. The reason why the current structure of our government does not allow fiscal efficiency is because it was not designed to do so.

BLUEPRINT FOR CHANGE

What is presented in this chapter is a blueprint for structural change in government. If we are to become serious about managing our physical and social resources more effectively, we must become serious about changing the structure of government and modernizing our institutions to make them more relevant to the people they are intended to serve.

Let's start with the premise that we actually need government, if for no other reason than to keep some form of social order. Beyond the provision of essential services, however, we must decide upon the degree to which government should act primarily as a regulatory authority and the degree to which it should further empower itself to intervene directly in the lives of its citizens.

INTERVENTIONIST GOVERNMENT

Interventionist government has been the norm at all levels in the Canadian federation, at least since the Second World War. The result has been an evolving "social contract" between our government and its citizens, which is founded (1) upon basic principles, such as those now found within the Charter of Rights and Freedoms guaranteeing Canadi-

26

ans equality and individual justice, (2) upon a universal and portable health care system, (3) upon free access to public (K-12) education, and (4) upon a social safety net of pensions, unemployment insurance and welfare to look after those who, for reasons beyond their control, require financial and other forms of assistance. What is clearly lacking in all of this, however, is a concomitant charter of individual responsibilities.

RESPONSIBILITIES IN A CARING SOCIETY

It can be argued (1) that since the nationalization of the Canadian Constitution and the introduction of the Charter of Rights and Freedoms in 1982, and probably for a decade or two before that, a growing percentage of our citizens have demonstrated glaring individual and collective irresponsibility by demanding that their governments provide a solution for every problem in their lives; (2) that when governments fail to address adequately the demands of particular special-interest groups, either for lack of programs or the money to deliver them, the resultant, orchestrated clamour is perceived as threatening a significant loss of public confidence in our institutions; and (3) that when politicians (most often in search of re-election) finally yield to whichever of these invariably costly, interventionist demands, they often do so by spending borrowed money—thus contributing to a spiraling public debt, and creating a cycle of dependence by fuelling demands for ever more interventionist schemes.

The dependence of our fellow citizens on government

programs must be broken, if only because government (albeit contrary to notions advanced in the popular press) cannot create the "caring" society they desire. One, it is altogether too expensive; two, this is not a role that government is very effective at fulfilling; and three, there may be a disproportionate price that all of us have to pay in diminished individual rights and freedoms. If our society is to continue to avoid debilitating moral decline, more of our people must be encouraged to take greater individual responsibility for looking after themselves, for members of their families, for people in their neighbourhoods and, in a broader sense, for the management of their communities.

Fortunately, Canadians still have a strong tradition of volunteerism to turn to. It is estimated that roughly half of every dollar that circulates within our economy does so through unpaid labour. Homemakers and volunteers who engage in community services through their church or non-profit societies have always played a vital role within the economy. A 1987 StatsCan "Survey of Volunteers" found one in four of our citizens over the age of fifteen—that is, 5.3 million Canadians—working in unpaid jobs without any expectation of monetary gain. The fact is that most of us want to help others. Indeed, StatsCan found a far higher rate of "job satisfaction" among volunteers (90%) than is usually obtained with a paid workforce.

StatsCan also discovered that female volunteers outnumber men, marrieds outnumber singles, that the volunteer rate is greater among people with higher education and incomes, and that almost half of our volunteers work with more than one charitable body. The average individual contribution was 191 hours per year; the total annual contribution was over a billion hours—the equivalent to 617,000 full-time jobs. In 1987, the total value of volunteer labour was estimated at $12 billion, which equaled about 43% of the total wages paid by all levels of government, the military included.

Distribution of Volunteers:

17% religious bodies, including services for the poor
16% sports and recreation
14% schools and community programs, nursery schools, camping trips
10% fund raising and help in hospitals, private homes, public events
9%   services for the homeless, abused women, and troubled young people
9%   service clubs, Red Cross, health, recreation, social service, cultural events
8%   community groups, minorities, the disabled, volunteer fire brigades
6%   employment counselling, consumer co-ops, tenant associations
4%   museums, libraries, art galleries, theatre groups, community newspapers
2%   environment, protection of animals
1%   crime prevention, legal aid, block parents, John Howard Society
1%   UNICEF, CARE, organizations for the third world

Of course, there are important individual benefits to be gained from being a volunteer: volunteers learn about organization, management, office and communication skills. In all of this, they develop confidence in their ability to handle problems, and what they learn may help them enter the labour force, or make them more valuable to their present employer. There are other benefits as well: according to a number of studies, volunteers live longer, healthier lives. And all of this without government intervention! Obviously, we need more of the same.

Only where the delivery of service to the public is deemed to be essential, and the cost is higher than could reasonably be expected to be recovered through private enterprise, does government have a legitimate role to play. The most oft-cited example here is social assistance. Our society has long prided itself on its protection of the poor, the disabled, and the aged. Although it is worth noting that the StatsCan Survey cited above confirms that the traditional role of the various churches in providing shelter, food, and clothing for the poor still exists, the sad fact is that the church has neither the influence nor the capacity to perform the function that today is demanded of the state in this regard. Public transit, ferries, along with educational and health care services, are further examples where government involvement is necessary to protect the interests of its citizens.

While the public may accept direct state intervention in such services as social welfare, health, education, and public transportation, there is a growing intolerance of those government services that can be provided by small business investors or community-based, non-profit organizations. The basic premise of this book, and of the philosophy that underlies the Progressive Democratic Alliance as a political movement, is that the power of the state should be put more properly into balance with the individual rights of its citizens. Governments should be empowered to regulate, but rarely should they administer the delivery of programs beyond essential services.

THE ROLE OF GOVERNMENT

However, it is more than ironic that we often focus our criticisms on the poor when we complain about the level of government expenditures. It is not single mothers on welfare who created billions of dollars of national debt. It is not the young person with a university degree, working for minimum wage at Canadian Tire, who has pushed the provincial debt to $28 billion dollars, with annual servicing costs of roughly $1.5 billion. Although income assistance, education and health care remain the biggest dollar items within government, there has been a general trend toward increased public borrowing for highways, ferries, and other capital construction that has pushed the debt level far beyond acceptable limits—as have the corporate-welfare practices of a succession of past, so-called "free enterprise" governments, which have thwarted individual initiative and free access to the market place through special deals, partnerships, subsidies, low- or no-interest loans, financial guarantees, purchasing and marketing arrangements, and straight handouts to financial and political backers. Ironically, this form of "*private enterprise* government", transcends the normal split between the so-called socialist and capitalist parties, because both have their own list of supporters who benefit first from the largesse of government.

Clearly, the last thing we need in British Columbia is to finance a bloated government on borrowed money. Quite the reverse is required: less government, the elimination of special status and privilege for some over others, restricted borrowing, and a reduction in tax demand. The Progressive Democratic Alliance is committed to a *free enterprise* government. Our stated goal is to provide the opportunity for more people to keep a little more of the money they earn, so that we can start to break their dependency on the state, and enhance individual initiative.

A REDUCTION IN TAXES

There is a credibility problem with politicians who state that they plan to reduce taxes. Most voters don't believe that they will live long enough see a political leader actually do this. Yet, reducing taxes is precisely what we *must* do if our economy is to grow. Only when government takes less money from working people will there be an increase in real wealth within the province. Because people with greater disposable incomes will spend and invest more within the communities in which they live, the net effect will be increased economic activity that creates more local jobs—thus creating a bigger pool of money from which taxes may be claimed.

As things stand today, those at the lower end of the income scale are becoming less able to make ends meet. What is more, they are losing confidence in their ability ever to get ahead, because the more they earn, the more government taxes them. Indeed, the ever-increasing demand of government for more tax revenue acts as a disincentive for many who might otherwise enter the workforce. In fact, if taxes are not reduced, fewer people will be prepared, or able, to provide for themselves through personal initiative and will be inextricably caught in the vicious cycle of dependency earlier described.

What the Progressive Democratic Alliance believes it can achieve through a significant reduction in provincial taxation is a society where fewer people are dependent upon government for income assistance, and where fewer people are unable to pay into the tax pool. In our socioeconomic model, the tax pool is bigger and deeper. Even though an individual's personal contribution will be less than he or she is paying now, revenue to government will be maintained. It might even expand, thereby allowing government to cut taxes further, especially if this cut were combined with the legislation to tie government spending to a fixed percentage of provincial gross domestic product—something that would put into perspective just what government can afford, and might cause public advocacy groups to tailor their demands accordingly.

A FOUR POINT PLAN FOR TAX RELIEF

As suggested above, the greatest contribution that government can make toward increasing employment is to put in place a comprehensive package of tax reforms that will have at its foundation a shift away from consumptive tax toward a single graduated tax on income. Indeed, I believe that the need to move toward a simplified tax that is more equitable than the current complex system is so important that the province should be prepared to move unilaterally if Ottawa fails to agree.

The tax system proposed by the Progressive Democratic Alliance has as its goal to (1) exempt those who earn less than $18,000, (2) place a 22% tax against those who earn between $18,000 and $32,000, (3) tax at a 24% rate those earning between $32,000 and $60,000, and (4) impose a flat 26% rate against those who earn more than $69,000.

The second and third planks in our tax reform plan have to do with property. We believe that it is important for British Columbians to be able to afford to buy their own homes. Consequently, on taking into consideration the increases in bank rates, the demand for huge downpayments, and the rising price of property, we have concluded that there must be tax relief on housing. We propose that the interest paid on a first mortgage of a primary residence be an allowable deduction against income. This would also apply to those who are renters. In both cases there would have to be a maximum value placed on what is deductible to prevent individuals using their mortgage to get interest refunded loans for consumer goods.

With a similar end goal, we would remove capital improvements on the land from property tax. Tax on capital improvements constitutes a tax on wealth, which is punitive. It is also unfair to seniors living on fixed incomes, who have their homes as their retirement projects, if it forces them to move out of their communities because they cannot meet the tax demand.

Fourth, we would remove education as an isolated tax on residential property owners in favour of a more equitable distribution of the tax burden to include all commercial, professional and industrial tax payers, who to date have avoided this most necessary funding priority.

Along with this four point plan for tax relief, the Progressive Democratic Alliance proposes incentive programs to enhance the opportunities for BC small business. Sales tax should be phased out for all products produced or assembled in BC. Further, there should be a two year tax holiday for BC small business that is posting a profit but directing those funds into BC backed business ventures. This last proposal to enhance the opportunities for small business operating within the province is a critical component of the tax relief program, because BC small business is our best hope for creating new jobs.

WHO'S RESPONSIBLE FOR JOB CREATION?

Let's be clear from the start. Government should not be held responsible for job creation. Jobs will be created when there is an opportunity for profit to be made within an open market, or when there is a need for a service within a community. The only permanent employment that government can "create" is in the civil service. While the economic benefit from public sector jobs is very real in terms of the movement of wealth, they do not create wealth, and any significant increase in these positions can only come with a concomitant increase in taxes.

Yet, politicians frequently promise jobs to the voters. In fact, one of the biggest challenges faced by a politician is to avoid playing this gambit at election time. "Promise them anything that will get you elected" is the code of the "backroom boys". Of course, the "chicken in every pot" (in modern language, "a high paying job for every citizen") style of politician has been with us for as long as we have had elected representatives. Today's electorate, however, is better educated and more informed than ever before. They have grown weary of politicians' lies, and are cynical about much of what they hear during the heat of an election campaign. And that's a problem, because it is only during an election that a real opportunity to make a choice is available. Without an honest approach to the issues by those seeking public office, people often cast their ballots as a protest against the party or individual they like the least, rather than voting for a specific set of policies. What is worse is that when a clear plan is presented, chances are it will not be believed.

The contradiction here is that because everyone wants a job that pays a reasonable, livable wage, and because politicians of all stripes have, over the course of time, been quick to pledge that, if elected, their administration will "create jobs", the public has developed the conviction that government *is* responsible for job creation. The fact that these promised jobs have but infrequently materialized seems to make no difference. Consequently, a reality check might be in order before you vote yet again for the politician who makes such an unrealistic and irresponsible promise.

CONTENDING POLITICAL APPROACHES

The NDP, as intimated, believes that government should meet the public's demands for increased services through borrowed capital, and programs administered through new and costly Crown Corporations, such as Forest Renewal BC, which was created in 1994 to "revitalize" the forest sector through enhanced silviculture and replanting contracts. In this example, the government has not only entered into direct competition with the private sector, which was previously responsible for tree-planting contracts, it has redirected stumpage fees from general revenues into the creation of an unnecessary administrative structure in order to do so.

In 1995, the NDP borrowed over $2.4 billion to fund the programs of its various Crown Corporations. The net result, according to the government, will be increased capital assets that will enhance BC's position with international money lenders. The reverse, however, seems to be taking place, as credit rating agencies are beginning to worry about our increasing debt-to-population ratio.

Further costly bureaucracy is the infrastructure Crown Corporations are most adept at creating, into which ever-increasing amounts of taxpayers' money will have to be allocated—money for which you and I are ultimately responsible. Forest Renewal BC, the Columbia Power Corporation, the Transportation Financing Authority, and BC 21 are but four new additions to the family of BC Crown Corporations, which includes, among others, the giant Insurance Corporation of British Columbia and BC Hydro. And then, of course, there are the quasi-governmental agencies for which we are responsible, such as the Workers' Compensation Board.

One, however, would be hard pressed to point to the former "free enterprise" Social Credit government, which concentrated all decision-making powers within Cabinet, as a model of fiscal responsibility. In 1990/91, their last year of government, Socred deficit spending ran to about $2.3 billion dollars. The new provincial Reform party promises no better, which is not surprising because all of its MLAs sat as Social Credit Members of the Legislature until the spring of 1994.

Neither do the provincial Liberals under Gordon Campbell offer much in the way of hope. The infusion of many, if not most, of the former Social Credit power brokers into this once noble party seems to have resulted in a total confusion of fiscal policy. Campbell says the Liberals will not spend beyond revenue, a policy to be enforced through balanced budget legislation. Just how that is to work, he has not said, except that each Cabinet Minister will be *personally* liable for any debt incurred in his or her Department—a proposal so ridiculous that he may have a tough time getting anyone to take a Cabinet post, should he ever be called upon to form a government. Under the Campbell scheme, former Social Services Minister Joan Smallwood would have been personally liable for a debt of about $19 million due to cost overruns in the 1993/4 fiscal year! Campbell's proposal is not only laughable, a commitment to spend only on the basis of revenue would halt most hospital, road, and school construction in the province. There are essential capital projects that require longer-term financing.

The approach adopted by the Progressive Democratic Alliance is to establish a single spending authority called the *Ministry of the Exchequer* to administer a BC Capital Financing Authority. This Ministry would be strictly controlled, and would be empowered to borrow for necessary capital construction, but only to a maximum of 5.0% of total budgeted annual expenditure, less any projected deficit. These capital construction projects would be administered by the Exchequer through publicly tendered contracts that favour the employment of local, skilled trades.

Although the Progressive Democratic Alliance's plan also calls for a move toward balanced budgets, we have taken what we believe to be a more realistic approach than other parties to the proposition, recognizing that if we are to balance revenue with expenditures, we must remove current duplications in bureaucracy and maximize the effective delivery of service to the public with less administrative and associated costs. We have largely rejected the drastic cut-backs approach taken by Alberta Premier Ralph Klein, despite the fact that he has achieved some major government cost-cutting. The Klein approach was so detrimental to the delivery of health services, for example, that he had to back away from his initiative in late 1995 in favour of more realistic expenditures. The Progressive Democratic Alliance regards health care, education, a reformed justice system, and a sound social safety net as government priorities.

THE EXCHEQUER

The Ministry of the Exchequer, referred to above, will bring together the Ministry of Finance, Treasury Board, the Assessment authority, and Audit Services into a single spending authority to more effectively control spending, and to establish government priorities. Of particular importance to the success of this new Ministry will be the mandate of the Assessment Authority to provide government with quarterly statements of revenue from all sources (this is in addition to concerning itself with the value of a reformed property tax system). Consequently, the government will be armed with more accurate projections of the money coming in, and will be able to adjust its spending accordingly. On the other side of the ledger, quarterly audits will allow the office of the Auditor General to provide the government ongoing value-for-money evaluations throughout the year—a vast improvement over the current practice of tabling such reports in the year following the actual expenditures. This would facilitate the elimination of government's most wasteful habits before they had a chance to be incorporated in yet another budget.

A single spending authority is only one part of the Progressive Democratic Alliance's plan to restructure government. In every case, the basic principle is to create greater efficiency and to guard against potential abuse of the public trust. No matter which political party may take office, the welfare, not just of this generation, but of future generations will be entrusted to it. The greatest threats to the wealth of the next generation are the short-sighted policies of the current one. Consequently, to remove the temptation for partisan or special interest spending by our elected representatives, there should be less discretion given to government over the spending of public money.

THE INTEGRATION OF MINISTRIES

The model for reform that we propose would take the eighteen line Ministries and put them into seven principal Ministries, with associated secretariats that would function within those seven Ministries. The result would be a streamlined and more efficient delivery of services through the reduction of duplication within government. What follows is a schematic diagram of our proposal for government, next to the model that is currently in place.

NEW INTEGRATED PDA
EXECUTIVE COUNCIL

PREMIER
Chair, Executive Council
International trade
Constitutional Issues

EXCHEQUER
Finance
Crown Corporations
Audit Services
Assessment Authority

ATTORNEY GENERAL
(independent from Cabinet)
Justice
Human Rights
Gaming
Arbitration services
Aboriginal Affairs
Labour Relations
Consumer Services
Multiculturalism
Ombudsman

**COMMUNITY
DEVELOPMENT**
Education
Advanced Education
Apprenticeships
Health

Social Services
Advocacy Assistance
Transit
Housing
Seniors

**ENVIRONMENTAL
SECRETARIAT**
Mining
Energy
Forestry
Crown Lands
Agriculture
Fisheries
Water
Environmental Standards
Wildlife
Air Quality

**REGIONAL
DEVELOPMENT**
Municipal Affairs
Regional Districts
Transportation and
Highways
Small Business
Economic Development
Tourism

CURRENT EXECUTIVE COUNCIL

PREMIER
(includes international trade).

ATTORNEY GENERAL
(includes Solicitor General and Justice)

MINISTRIES
Finance

Employment and Investment

Aboriginal Affairs

Forests

Environment Lands and Parks

Agriculture and Fisheries

Municipal Affairs

Government Services

Energy, Mines and Petroleum Resources

Highways

Housing

Women's Equality

Skills, Labour and Training

Tourism and Culture and Small Business

Education

Health

DOWNSIZING THE BUREAUCRACY

Restructuring the operation of government in BC will result in a dramatically reduced bureaucracy over the long term, with smaller staff cuts in the early stages of implementation. It will take two years to fully integrate Ministries, as legislative redrafting and physical relocation take place. In some instances, there will be relocation of existing employees, whose responsibilities will change; in others, positions will be eliminated. However, this downsizing of the bureaucracy will be accomplished in a humane manner, taking into consideration the lives of those who will be affected.

It is estimated that roughly 12% of existing staff positions will be eliminated as integration occurs, and that the numbers within some areas of the civil service will continue to be reduced through attrition, early retirement, and incentive programs such as those used in the private sector. Duties will change for many classes of employees, getting them out from behind their desks and into the field, where they can directly interact with the people they serve.

AN IMPORTANT NEW ROLE FOR MLAS

Under this proposed restructuring, each Ministry contains a number of secretariats, to which MLAs will be assigned to assist the responsible Minister. These secretariats, empowered to assist in the decentralization of services to the regions of the province, will provide an important opportunity for elected Members to interface with government on behalf of their constituents. In the current system, those

MLAs on the government side of the House who are not in Cabinet are faced with the prospect of spending most of their time warming seats on the backbenches, occasionally hurling personal insults across a partisan Legislative floor in what passes for legislative debate, and of trying to "sell" their government's unpopular decisions to their constituents when the Legislature is not in session.

A LAZY LEGISLATURE ADDRESSED

British Columbia has the laziest Legislature in the country, sitting, as it normally does, only during a Spring Session that lasts little more than three months. The Progressive Democratic Alliance is committed to change this. It is our view that the role of the Legislature is not well understood by the general public, and that, in consequence, it has become somewhat irrelevant to the "average" British Columbian. There may be some interest in the Throne Speech's outline of the government's legislative program at the opening of each Session, or in how much taxes have increased when the Budget is brought down, but that is about it.

Instead of leaving the timing of Legislative sittings and elections to the whim of Cabinet, the Progressive Democratic Alliance advocates the introduction of legislation requiring both a Spring Session and a Fall Session of the Legislature, as well as fixed sitting days. To further restrict political opportunism on the part of the government, we also advocate a fixed four-year term for the Legislature, and a fixed provincial election day.

A FIXED SPRING BUDGET DAY

Historically, BC's budget has been brought down by government sometime before the first day of April, which is the first day of the new fiscal year. But that has not always been the case. During the last Social Credit government in the late '80s and early '90s, there were instances of May budgets. The principal reason to implement a fixed Spring Budget Day is to remove uncertainty from the marketplace, and to provide public institutions an easier job in planning their fiscal year. Every hospital, school, college, university, and crown corporation, as well as many non-profit societies, are directly dependent upon the government for their money. And it is grossly unfair, inefficient, and costly for them to be obliged to begin spending money in a new fiscal year for which they have no final budget. Also, because this money is so important within each community in BC, virtually every business, especially every small business, is also either directly or indirectly affected—as are all of us, in large or small measure, by any alteration in the tax rate.

SPECIAL WARRANT SPENDING

When the government has not managed to table a budget before April, it resorts to a practice (much frowned upon) called *Special Warrant* spending. What this amounts to is Cabinet approving behind closed doors the spending of public money—money that has not been included within any budget and therefore has not been approved by the

Legislature in the *Estimates Debate,* which involves a detailed examination of every Ministry's proposed expenditures. Special Warrants is an anti-democratic practice that gives the government the opportunity to spend our money without legislative scrutiny.

BEYOND THE DEBATES

Most people are sufficiently acquainted with the process of passing bills into law, even when the Legislature of their province and the Parliament of their country seem far distant and irrelevant to their lives. They may even know that majority governments are most often elected dictatorships that seldom tolerate interference with their legislative agendas. That said, I think it fair to say that, through sheer grit and determination, BC's two Progressive Democratic Alliance MLAs were able to force the NDP government to withdraw and redraft its Human Rights legislation, which threatened the fundamental right to free expression in our society. The government's amendments to the Human Rights Code were well-intended, but heavy-handed in that they would have curtailed freedom of speech by imposing the highly subjective judgements of a government-appointed Commission on questions of what did or did not constitute hate literature. Our position was that we already had laws against the dissemination of hate literature, and courts that were competent to rule on such matters, and that what was being proposed went beyond the established and accepted restrictions on these materials.

The introduction of "bubble zones" around govern-ment-funded abortion clinics, passed in 1995, was another piece of NDP legislation we opposed. In this case, the right of assembly was removed, and the right to silent protest pro-hibited. Although we failed to prevent the passage of the bill, it is important to note that the debates in the Legisla-ture proved useful in a successful court challenge in January of 1996 to this legislation, as did the Progressive Democratic Alliance's philosophical position on civil rights.

The point that I want to make in this section, however, is that the language and passage of legislation is only one part of the process of governance. Often far more important are the regulations which enable the state to implement the intent of the bill. For example, if a particular Act prescribes a fine for any violation of its terms, the regulation will state the amount, how that fine is served on an individual, and what rights that individual has within the law to protest. Generally, the first time the public or the elected Members encounter new regulations is when they are confronted with them in action.

Any time politicians are given power to invoke or revise legislation without the benefit of debate or scrutiny by Opposition Members, problems arise. And the ability to set regulations to govern the administration of Acts is only one discretionary power that a government enjoys. Orders in Council, which may be described as votes within Cabinet, are another, wherein the Ministers of the Crown are granted sweeping powers to make far-reaching decisions. For exam-ple, the Ministers may issue licenses for wood harvest, spend money outside of the approved budget, or give authority to themselves to borrow from various lenders. It is this power that allows the corrupt, who seek and sometimes obtain political office, to advance the interests of particular friends and insiders at the expense of the people who, in good faith, elected them. We need to establish a process of Open Government that removes any possibility for members of the Executive Council (the Premier and Cabinet) to direct spending and policy without the benefit of parliamentary debate.

REMOVING POLITICAL INTERFERENCE

The spending priorities of government must be set with a view to providing, on a fair and equal basis, revenue to all regions of the province based on responsible planning and need. Consequently, partisan discretionary spending will have to be abolished. The objective here is to stop an NDP, Social Credit, Liberal, or other traditional party-type governments from favouring ridings held by one of their Members. To achieve this, MLAs must shed their partisan coats and leave them at the door when entering the halls of government. In return, we must recognize, perhaps for the first time, that every MLA, regardless of the party to which he or she belongs, is an important part of government, and that serious discussions and decisions on public business should not be the exclusive preserve of MLAs whose party holds the majority of seats in the Legislature.

To suggest that elected representatives focus their concerns and energies on their individual ridings and the interests of their constituents, rather than on the political fortunes of the parties that nominated them, is to propose a revolutionary change of perspective for most MLAs. The Progressive Democratic Alliance, however, believes that this is essential to reforming the process of government in British Columbia. And to reinforce this concept in the Legislature, we will seat MLAs by region, rather than by party. At present, government and opposition MLAs are seated in an arcane, adversarial arrangement, facing each other across the floor of the Legislature at a distance of two sword lengths. It is time to create a less partisan Chamber, where the politicians can focus on accomplishing things for their constituents, as opposed simply to vying for the attention of the press gallery, often allowing themselves to be made objects of public ridicule in the process.

With MLAs seated by region, representing the broad-based interests of their constituencies, there will be genuine opportunity to canvass issues with the Executive Council without the interference of partisan politics. Each Ministry and its secretariats will be able to work with the MLAs of all parties in serving the broad-based interests of the public.

ELECTORAL REFORM

Of course, the wisdom in changing the traditional seating arrangement in the Legislature will be better seen after an Electoral Reform Commission has redrawn the province's electoral boundaries, reducing the number of ridings from

75 to 51, and creating a better balance in representation between the Lower Mainland and the interior and northern regions of the province. What the Progressive Democratic Alliance is proposing is that the Electoral Reform Commission be mandated to devise a formula that would weigh population, geographic area, and the percentage of popular vote received by registered political parties, in deciding representation in the Legislative Assembly.

Although this proposition will be attacked because it compromises the democratic principle of representation by population, the reality is that because BC has a resource-based economy, most of our real wealth comes from the province's rural interior and north. Only a fraction of our wealth is generated in the urban triangle, comprising Greater Vancouver, Victoria and Nanaimo, which dominates the Legislature by electing the majority of the MLAs. If, however, in the final analysis there is sufficient public opposition to change from a strict "rep by pop" formula, the terms of reference provided this Electoral Reform Commission must be broad enough to introduce at least limited proportional representation by assigning a fixed number of seats to those parties that receive five or more percent of the popular vote in any general election.

DECENTRALIZATION OF SERVICES

Accompanying this thrust toward regional representation in the Legislature must be a real commitment to the decentralization of decision-making when it comes to delivering services to our various communities—something that would reduce the growing cynicism of people toward the way the government spends their hard-earned tax dollars. By passing some of the authority for allocation of government resources to the community, the Progressive Democratic Alliance would enlist local input and expertise in making more efficient use of public funds.

This approach is the opposite of what we experienced in the dying days of the Harcourt government, where school districts have been forcibly integrated to create a more centralized system, and Regional Health Boards have had to adjust their geographic boundaries to meet the needs of the Victoria bureaucracy. In these examples, the government in Victoria imposed its views on the allocation of resources on local communities and jurisdictions, rather than allowing them to help direct the funding of services.

MORE OPEN GOVERNMENT

It is important to entrench within the new government model we are developing an increased level of empowerment for the population at large, so that, among other considerations, the process of government is made more relevant to their daily lives. The Progressive Democratic Alliance proposes a provincial registry be struck to include the names of all bona fide, BC lobby, interest, and community groups, with a view to establishing a process of *direct delegation*, whereby these organizations would be provided opportunity to come directly onto the floor of the Legislature to present, in the form of white papers, *initiatives* they wished the government to entertain as legislation. Once a delegation had made its presentation, the Legislature would debate and vote on a resolution either to draft the white paper in question into the form of a bill, to send it for further review and drafting to a Standing Committee of the Legislature, or to terminate further discussion.

Such a process would provide all legitimate groups, and not just those with the ear of a particular party in government, with an avenue to the halls of power. It would also provide them an opportunity to be heard by both the politicians and the population at large. If their initiative had merit, it would be difficult for the government to stonewall the issue. Finally, by creating a somewhat more level playing field for BC lobby, interest, and community groups, it would serve to limit the backroom power of the political insider.

At present, companies know that their welfare is affected by the direction and policy of government, and they also know that politicians need money to print their brochures, buy their TV time, and run their radio ads. The consequence of this knowledge is a political lobby which can undermine the practice of government of, for, and by the people.

POLITICAL FUNDING

An ideal political funding system would permit people to contribute only a limited amount of money for tax credit, but would, in consequence, encourage as many people as possible to become involved in the political process. The Progressive Democratic Alliance, for example, is promoting a direct support system with each party member encouraged to contribute a nominal amount of ten or twenty-five dollars per month. While we do not turn away larger donors, we do not make a direct pitch to them either. In principle, the broader the base of support, the better financed the party, and, I believe, the more democratic the process that supports politics and politicians throughout the province. What is more, if all of the donations are made public by law, the secrecy and manipulation of the backroom will be broken, and a healthier system will be created.

British Columbia now enjoys a new Elections Act that will regulate and strictly limit future political spending. While the Opposition and Government parties each claim to support the full disclosure of all campaign contributions and contributors, the fact is that when most of these politicians have had the opportunity to disclose, they have opted not to. Gordon Campbell is a case in point: he has steadfastly refused to identify the contributors to his 1993 campaign to gain the leadership of the BC Liberals.

Since entering politics, I have firmly held the view that any politician who accepts large donations from a limited number of sources will become beholden to them. I offer, as a personal example, an incident that happened during the public debates that preceded the national referendum on the Charlottetown Accord in 1992, when I was in the middle of a fund-raising campaign among the leaders of business and industry in Vancouver. At the time, as Leader of the

Official Opposition, I was the only prominent politician in British Columbia who had begun speaking to the details of the Accord from the "No" side. Readers will recall that the major national political parties, various provincial governments, including ours in British Columbia, the national and provincial media (CKNW's Rafe Mair excepted), the CEOs of our national banks, leaders of industry, in fact the entire Canadian establishment, were firmly in support of the "Yes" campaign. It was the view of these lions of insider thinking that I should not undertake support of the "No" side. In the event, I'd just completed a "productive" fundraising breakfast, and had returned to my office, when I received a phone call from one of our new donors:

> "Gordon, I just heard on the radio that you're supporting the 'No' campaign. That really pisses me off. If I don't hear by tomorrow morning that you have re-considered, I will put a stop payment on that four-digit cheque."

Within half an hour of that phone call, I had traced his cheque, and had my staff return it by courier, with the message: "Don't try to buy me, I am not for sale."

VOTER RESPONSIBILITY

The challenge to build a new engine of government is not an easy one, and it will take direct action against the power brokers who have for so long controlled our province. To that end this book is written, and to that end I labour on.

Ultimately, those voters who supported me in the 1991 provincial election, and who shared my concern over the Charlottetown Accord in 1992, will again decide my fate.

PAYING
THE PRICE:

WELFARE, EDUCATION, AND HEALTH CARE

OUR SAFETY NET

Among the qualities that distinguish us from our American cousins is our adherence to *three basic guarantees* provided each individual in Canadian society. The first, which is no doubt rooted in the experience of our seniors with the Great Depression of the 1930s, is our commitment to the maintenance of a state-supported "social safety net" to care for those who, for reasons beyond their control, require income and other assistance. The second, which finds origin in the 19th century establishment of a system of tax-supported elementary education in Ontario, Nova Scotia, and British Columbia, is our belief that all citizens have a right to publicly funded education up to the completion of grade 12 (which some would argue should be extended through university). Finally, but by no means least in importance, is our demand that everyone have access to comprehensive and affordable medical and hospitalization insurance, which we fondly call our universal health care system—something that has been a full, and much-prized Canadian reality since 1972.

Unfortunately, these basic Canadian social guarantees are threatened today by the federal government's response to its deficit and debt crisis, which in part involves keeping for its own purposes an increasing share of the tax dollars it previously collected and "transferred" back to the provinces for the administration and delivery of social services and health care, as well as for higher, technical, ESL, and French-language education. Because the present welfare, health and education features of our common Canadian existence consume over seventy percent of the annual provincial budget in British Columbia—expenditures that, in large measure, are required by law—the result of Ottawa's financial finagling is simply to dump our share of its problems on the steps of the BC Legislature, thus creating a situation in which we may have no choice but to scrap present federal-provincial tax-sharing arrangements.

The recent rise of the "radical right" in Canada has spawned a breed of politician (and I include in that category the post-1993, Mulroney-style Liberals in British Columbia) who panders to the worst instincts of the electorate at large by attacking those on income and social assistance, bashing away at our teachers, and advocating that we start to pare down our publicly funded health care system by creating a rather dubious distinction between vital services and those that are not considered to be essential. This, of course, has been a deleterious addition to the previously mentioned, active debate among BC politicians on future operating and capital funding for our schools and hospitals, given a general commitment to provincial deficit and debt reduction.

It takes a particularly principled politician to stick to his or her philosophical positions when these seem less than "bankable" in terms of voter support. For example, the NDP government in BC has found it expedient to take a position on welfare questions which is more in line with those of the radical-right Reform and Liberal parties than it is with their own platform or 1991 election promises. To be sure, there are those who seek to defraud the welfare system in British Columbia, and there are some who have become quite proficient at doing so. Certainly, we must ensure that the system is at all times properly monitored, and that we respond immediately by having the small minority who offend against it criminally charged. However, we would do well always to remember that the majority of people who are receiving money through our welfare system are children.

WHAT ABOUT THE CHILDREN?

In my life, I have been most fortunate to have been able to raise two wonderful children, Christina and Mathew. Now in their twenties and able to look after their own interests, these well-rounded individuals are able to make what they will of their lives. After my marriage to Judi, I became step-

59

father to three more wonderful children: Tanita, Kiri, and Kas, born in 1992, 1990, and 1988, respectively. They too are children who are fortunate to have available to them, especially when in our care, tremendous opportunities to travel, meet new people, learn about their province and country, and establish in their minds career horizons that they will, if they apply themselves, attain. More importantly, none of our five children will ever have to worry that they will not have good clothing, food on the table, or a chance for higher education, because both Judi and I have had the opportunity to pursue an education, and have the necessary lifeskills and resources to make a secure living. But our family is becoming less typical of the majority of people who live within the ranks of the so-called middle class in Canada, and its example offers a striking contrast to the problems of those who constitute the poor among us.

Far too many children are born into, or fall into, the web of welfare or state support. Indeed, many grow up in an environment of constant stress and concern about the provision of adequate food, shelter and clothing. Or, they so lack the love and attention they need that they end up on our streets, fending for themselves and each other. These young people, through no fault of their own, have limited opportunity to secure even a reasonably basic education and, consequently, have very restricted career horizons.

In my capacity as an MLA, I have had the good fortune to meet many professionals and volunteers involved in youth-work, and almost to a person they tell me that young people at all levels of society today share a common fear for their futures in a world where opportunities for decent, long-term jobs are scarce, where the cost of living is skyrocketing, where natural resources are being depleted, and where the entire global environment is seriously threatened. They also tell me that our youth seem highly cynical that anyone can, or will, do anything to change this situation.

It has become clichéd to say that our children represent our future but, cliché or not, this is true, and we must focus our time and attention on the needs of our province's children. Clearly, the first objective of a compassionate society is to ensure that there is a social safety net in place that will ensure all children and youth the material support essential to physical survival, without unduly compromising their individual dignity as human beings in the process. The second objective is to design the social safety net so that it provides opportunity for each individual to advance out of the "welfare web" of food banks and income support. A good system provides a hand *up*, not a *handout*.

THE PERSPECTIVE OF OUR ELDERS

Unfortunately, the radical right has found a ready audience for its message of intolerance and reaction among those of our citizens now approaching retirement age, a message that encourages them to selectively remember being able to go out and "make it" on their own, and to dismiss as groundless the fears of our younger generation that there may be no, or at best a limited future left for them. Some of our elders too often forget that the decent-paying jobs available to them in the affluent, immediate post-World War II period, where mass production and labour-intensive industries thrived, no longer exist. The reality in post-Free Trade Canada is that jobs that pay more than the minimum wage are hard to find, and that job security is rare—unless you can land a government job which is not subject to cutbacks, or belong to a strong union such as the United Food and Commercial Workers.

What is more, a significant percentage of our elders refuse to acknowledge that the social mores of their generation may no longer be relevant—mores stereotyped in the popular sitcoms of the '50s and '60s like *Leave it to Beaver* and *Father Knows Best*—which supported a rigidly structured home environment centred on a nuclear family, with a stay-at-home mom, and a working dad who kept the same job for thirty or forty years. Certainly, they find it difficult even to consider that their much vaunted thrifty spending habits may well have resulted from the absence of readily available credit. No wonder they have a hard time accepting the emergence of a new social order, in which a growing percentage of the students in our public school system come from "mixed" families, where the moms and dads, who both have to work outside the home just to make ends meet, are on their second or third marriage, and where single parents are common.

The reader shouldn't misunderstand what is meant here. I am not arguing that the social mores of the 1990s are better than those of the 1950s. But I am saying that they are different, and that to measure or, worse yet, judge today's youth by outdated standards will create more problems than it will solve. Not only are the young people of today frustrated by the seemingly insurmountable obstacles that face them, they also find themselves denied the approval of their elders in a situation beyond their control.

OPPORTUNITIES FOR GENERATION "R"

Recently, crossing from Gibsons to Horseshoe Bay on one of the BC Ferries, I was approached, as I frequently am, by a middle-aged constituent who recognised me and wanted to talk politics. Social services, this real estate agent told me, should be privatized: "If you let us entrepreneurs deal with the layabouts," he said, "we'd soon weed out the deadbeats that cost us all that money." My response was to ask him if he could tell me how much those "dead beats" actually cost the taxpayer each year, and the extent to which his lot would improve if these people were off the welfare roles. Of course, he didn't know exactly, but he was sure that it cost him "millions". He was right. In fact, the answer is about $300 million. To give this a little perspective, however, this figure is equal to roughly half of the uncollected debt that government has on its books in each fiscal year—debt in large measure put there by an entirely different class of "welfare bums", some of whom no doubt were within the circle of my constituent's entrepreneurial acquaintance.

Now, I am not suggesting that we should accept welfare fraud—of any kind. Quite the contrary. But I am saying that we should also put the costs into perspective and recognize that solutions to the problems of our time, including those of the welfare web, can only be found through an approach to education at all levels that results in the creation of a more caring society. This means creating an educational system that is relevant to today's needs and values, not yesterday's, and rejecting the heavy hand of government in a dependent and punitive social system. The last thing we need is a system where the laws of intolerance are enforced in what will amount to a police state. Only a civilized approach to solving social problems with social solutions offers hope for tomorrow.

EDUCATION: THE SECOND GUARANTEE

A sound public education system is the second guarantee that all Canadians enjoy. Like our other rights and privileges, however, education has become one of the more contentious matters in today's public arena. And front and centre in all of this are those who would dismantle our system of public education in favour of a private system which would "go back to" a more fundamental instructional focus, commonly referred to as "the three Rs": reading, writing and arithmetic.

Because there are a number of approaches to this subject, it is important to begin by making a distinction between the more prominent of the alternatives. "Traditional Schools" are public schools, in which the curriculum and instructional model are traditional and teacher-driven. This is antithetical to the controversial student-driven approach of the ill-fated "Year 2000" teaching model, which was introduced by the former Social Credit government, and phased out in response to considerable public pressure by the present NDP government. Unfortunately, the public debate that resulted in the return to traditional schooling from a system that parents perceived as giving students too much power and control in the classroom also began the "Charter School" movement in British Columbia.

"Charter Schools" are advocated by people who claim that current public education system represents an unhealthy monopoly, and that public funding should be allocated to a private school model. They demand that the government pass legislation to allow these schools to opt out of regular school districts, and establish their own school boards. In effect, they advocate dismantling the public school system in British Columbia—something the Progressive Democratic Party strongly opposes.

THE FOUR BASICS

I can, however, understand the considerable frustration felt by parents who believe that our public education system is somehow failing their children. It is my belief that such "failure" as does exist within the system can be traced to the approach taken toward: (1) curriculum, (2) funding development, (3) contract negotiation, and (4) instructional currency.

Let's be clear: the reason why there are so many firmly held opinions on education is that we all have had, happily or otherwise, our own experience in school. And it is from that experience, whether or not it bears any relationship to what goes on in the classroom today, that these opinions are formulated. Of course, there are those property owners who resent the taxes they must pay to cover the high and tangible costs of education when they do not have children in the school system. With regard to this latter point, I have been arguing since I first entered politics in 1986 that education should be removed as an isolated tax on property. As earlier noted, the Progressive Democratic Alliance sees such a move as part of a comprehensive tax reform program that would more equitably spread the cost of education by collecting school taxes from industrial and commercial tax units, as well as from residential properties.

CURRICULUM AND TECHNOLOGY

On the matter of curriculum, there is a need to recognize that we are living in a very quickly changing world as far as technology is concerned. It is therefore critically important that there be recognition that literacy in the 1990s and through the first decade of the new century will not be limited to traditional definitions. Today's students will have to have access to, and be proficient in, the use of computers to permit them access to the information highway, and engage them directly in the world-network of knowledge exchange, or the World Wide Web (WWW), as it is called.

To this end, there is a need to create a BC Educational Advisory Council made up of representatives from the education faculties and various disciplines in our universities,

elected representatives from the BC Teachers Federation
and the BC School Trustees Association, a cross section of
parents from home and school associations, and staff from
the Ministry of Education. The purpose of this Educational
Advisory Council would be to ensure that the basics of education are combined with new technological advances and
with exposure to the realities of the changing workplace. In
this way, students will be adequately prepared for life after
graduation from grade twelve. This would also facilitate
long-term curriculum planning, and tie it to overall funding.
This new educational authority would cross-reference its
work with other Canadian jurisdictions to ensure that British
Columbia students are exposed so far as practical to curricu-
la similar to that in the rest of the country.

EDUCATION FUNDING

During the many public hearings of, and in the written sub-
missions presented to the Sullivan Commission of a few
years ago, the issue of educational funding assumed as high
a priority as the quality of the educational system. Indeed,
the one item that was consistently commented on was the
need to change the manner by which our schools are funded. At present, operational funding is provided to the school
boards from the budget of the Ministry of Education, and
capital funding through a crown corporation called "BC 21".
All budgets are set on an annual basis, but, as noted in the
previous chapter, sometimes funding announcements take
place when the province's fiscal year, which begins on April
1st, is already underway. A perennial problem in high-growth

districts is that school board funding often fails to include provision for those students who arrive just after September or January cutoff dates, and thus did not appear on the list of students used to calculate funding.

Currently, the Ministry of Education uses a funding formula for financing local school board operations based on the ratio between the number of students and the number of instructional and administrative personnel. That is to say it identifies the number of funded Full Time Equivalent (FTE) students in relation to the number of teachers and other educators (including administrators). There are several problems with this particular system, the most obvious of which is that, because the ratio is based on students and all of the teachers and administrators, the weighting is somewhat skewed. The larger problem, however, is the lack of long-term, secured financing which would allow school boards to plan strategically. Since my involvement in provincial politics, and during my tenure as President of the Faculty Association at Capilano College, I have repeatedly called for an end to formula funding based on FTEs, and the implementation of four-year-base-financing. A four-year-base-budget would provide school boards the necessary security to properly plan the long-term development of their district. Not only would they have the benefit of long-term operational dollars, they also would have the benefit of proper capital planning so that they could match construction of new school facilities with demand. This clearly would be much more cost-effective.

A PUBLIC BUILDING DESIGN REGISTRY

Another idea that would reduce education capital costs by an immeasurable amount would be the standardisation of school building designs. In the recent Abbotsford by-election, the Progressive Democratic Alliance candidate, Cathy Goodfellow, introduced the concept of a government building design registry, which would remove the continual commissioning of architects and engineers to meet the same basic needs in each separate community. She found an overwhelming acceptance from a public that had been treated over the years to such a wide variety of designs for their schools—at huge costs to the taxpayer—that they welcomed her sensible approach to this question.

TEACHER BARGAINING MODELS

While secure finances are an important part of solving the problem of education delivery in British Columbia, so too is the need to secure and retain the best possible teachers within all our schools, and particularly within those schools in the interior and the north of our province. With that in mind, it is timely to comment on the move within this province since 1993 to remove community control from teacher bargaining in favour of a centralised system of "one size fits all". There are already rumblings in some school districts that the Employers Council, created by the NDP in the spring of 1994 to bargain on behalf of the BC School Trustees, will be too heavily weighted with representatives from the urban centres of the lower mainland, and will thus be dominated in its decision making by Vancouver.

SCHOOL DISTRICT AMALGAMATIONS

Certainly, the above situation will not be improved by the NDP government's decision to reduce the number of School Districts within the province from seventy-five to fifty-seven, through a process of amalgamation. While this approach will be welcome in some areas where the populations share common educational needs, and the geography of the region is conducive to ease of travel, there are other areas such as the Kootenays and Powell River/Sunshine Coast/Howe Sound where amalgamation makes no sense whatsoever.

What the Education Minister has said he is attempting to accomplish is a savings in administrative costs of roughly $30 million a year beginning in 1998/99, with further savings in long-term operational costs. This the Minister tells us he is going to accomplish without the loss of programs to students in the affected districts. A closer review of the situation, however, suggests otherwise. Even if all of the administration was to be removed from every district that is named for amalgamation, the resulting savings will not yield the desired amount. And it is certain that such savings cannot be accomplished without significant reductions in classroom programs. At a time when we should be placing education at the top of our priorities, this attempt at further centralization of delivery is unwise.

TEACHER-BASHING AND EDUCATION POLITICS

What is particularly interesting in the bi-polar politics of
British Columbia is the employment of teacher-bashing by
both the right and the left. Traditionally, it was the right-
wing politicians who used the teachers as their foil, whereas
the left-wing NDP always came to their defense. Thus it was
that in the general election of 1991, many teachers, who are
in a well-organized and often powerful union, worked for
the NDP. Some even ran for office and became MLAs. When
the educational debates began to heat up in 1992, and
became intense in 1993 with some teachers' strikes, however,
the NDP government moved swiftly to introduce back-to-
work legislation in an emergency vote, which removed collective bargaining rights from Teachers' Federation locals,
and created a new provincial bureaucracy on behalf of
school trustees.

The emergency debate, although rigidly controlled, was
a dramatic one. At the time, I was still Liberal leader, but
because the party was in the throes of replacing me with
Gordon Campbell, my Liberal colleagues in the Legislature
refused to allow me to speak during the debate. The point is,
that of all the MLAs from the three political parties in the
House at the time—NDP, Liberal, and Social Credit—I was
the only Member to vote against that bill. (My colleague Judi
Tyabji was back in her riding.) And if the Mulroney-style
provincial Liberals, who supported the government education agenda after the summer of 1993, had their way, they
would remove collective bargaining rights from teachers

altogether by declaring them an Essential Service. What is more, they would then start to eliminate school districts in order to consolidate control in the Minister's office.

The trouble with teacher-bashing, beyond the fact that it does a serious disservice to many honourable women and men, is that despite the limited political capital that might be gained, it does nothing to solve existing problems—and there are some real problems with our education system. Further, it lowers teacher morale, and often makes existing problems worse. Few people will ever realize from reading their newspapers that one of the more frequent issues in a teachers' strike is educational resources. When we ignore the input of our teachers, it may be our children who suffer the most.

A STUDENT-DRIVEN BUDGET

Because we all have had different experiences with schools and teachers, our opinions on what should be done to improve our educational system are about as varied as our experiences. Where I think we can agree, however, is on the question of prioritizing funding so that we can make better use of the money that we currently commit to education. As already explained, this will be greatly facilitated by the introduction of longer-term planning by school boards, and by returning to those boards local control over the delivery of education. In short, budgets should be student-driven, not driven by a theoretical formula that has little relevance to reality, and restricts the flexibility needed to plan properly over the long term.

The people in Powell River, for example, will remember only too well the bitter dispute that resulted in the work stoppage and school closure that took place in 1993. In part, the problem was caused by a school board forced to negotiate a contract that would have them commit to funding programs when they had no control over the receipt of the necessary funds. In fact, they didn't even know if the cost of the settlement they finally negotiated would be forthcoming from Victoria. And the public outside the Lower Mainland remembers just how quickly the NDP legislated teachers back to work when their job action affected Vancouver, and how students in the Kootenays, the North, and Powell River had to spend weeks trying to learn their lessons at home.

LOCAL BARGAINING RIGHTS

The NDP government's knee-jerk reaction to all of this was to remove local bargaining rights from school districts and to put everything into "one big pot". The bill effecting this centralization of bargaining was introduced during the Legislative Session of 1994 by Finance Minister Elizabeth Cull, one of the toughest of the NDP Cabinet Ministers. This legislation was clearly designed to please those in the public who had been calling for essential service designation for teachers. Under this new system of teacher bargaining, when one teacher is on strike, all of BC's teachers are on strike.

This means that Vancouver teachers could close every school in the province if they fail to reach agreement on a subject critical to Vancouver, but of limited interest beyond the Lower Mainland and southern Vancouver Island. English as a Second Language is one such example.

The better solution is to restore local control over budgets, give districts a four-year budget to work with, and foster a better working relationship among teachers, parents, and school trustees. It can be done, but it will take considerable political will to do so. The two sitting Members of the Progressive Democratic Alliance were the only two MLAs to take issue with the legislation that installed province-wide bargaining, and for all of the reasons outlined above.

HEALTH CARE: OUR THIRD GUARANTEE

Politicians today seem either to be leading a crusade to save our health care system, or leading the charge to dismantle its universality. Curiously, both campaigns seem to be premised on the assumption that our health care spending is out of control. And both are wrong! We do not have runaway health care costs. The fact is that the per capita cost of health delivery, which is the amount of money spent on direct services for each person, has remained relatively constant within the province in recent years. What has risen are administration costs that have resulted from a growing number of bureaucrats who have been hired to administer the system.

CLOSER TO HOME

The recent Seaton Commission into health care in British Columbia made recommendations with respect to the delivery of these services and to possible changes in administrative structure necessary to that delivery. "Closer to Home" was a catch phrase the Commission used to address the need to provide more services to clients of the system, either in their home or in an outpatient facility that would reduce significantly the need for long hospital stays, and therefore free up scarce hospital beds. These recommendations for a "New Direction" in health care were generally well received by health care providers and the public alike.

In 1993, the NDP government brought in health care legislation in response to the Seaton Commission Report, which focused on redesigning the administrative structure and decentralizing the delivery of health care services. Thus began the dismantling of the existing system of hospital boards in favour of Community Health Councils (CHCs) and Regional Hospital Boards (RHBs). The CHCs were to include a cross-section of community-based health care providers. The RHBs were to have 18 members: 6 elected by the public at large, 6 by the local health care providers, and 6 by Ministerial appointment. An important historical footnote is that the new administrative structure allowed for complete Ministerial appointments to the new councils and boards for the first five years.

These new bodies displaced the old hospital boards, which were elected by people who held membership cards in particular hospital societies. A number of these old boards, such as the one in Vernon, had become centres of political controversy, as right-wing, pro-life groups sought control of the boards to prevent abortions from occurring in their hospitals. This was a situation the NDP was committed to change. And naturally enough, the new councils and boards contained many appointees who favoured the NDP's health policies.

The time involved in the actual establishment of the Community Health Councils and Regional Hospital Boards varied from region to region in the province. Some communities already had associations which were similar to the structures being proposed, and could therefore be first through the gate. Others spent the first two years in large discussion groups trying to work out their terms of reference. By the fall of 1994, however, every community had a core group of dozens of volunteers who had spent considerable time and effort trying to implement the provisions of the legislation in the best interests of their community.

CONTENDING POLITICAL POSITIONS

The opposition Liberals under Gordon Campbell and the Reformers under Jack Weisgerber have stated that they will eliminate these new boards and councils if elected to government. Their position is that there has not been adequate discussion in communities about these bodies, which is blatantly untrue. Countless hours have been put in by hundreds of community volunteers, who have worked hard to try to sort out what the government was trying to accomplish under then Health Minister Elizabeth Cull. The Progressive Democratic Alliance also disagrees with the administrative structure as it stands, but would work to streamline it, rather than eliminate it and risk losing the constructive initiatives put in place by community representatives. We would like to reduce the number of members in some of the CHCs, which have run as high as 51. We would like to see all 18 RHB members elected by the public at large, using a Regional District model to ensure fair geographic-community representation. This streamlining, in addition to involving a devolution of power from the centralized control of the Minister into the communities, would result in a reduction in the size of the bureaucracy.

AN OUNCE OF PREVENTION

The NDP government has missed the boat in their health care initiatives in the area of preventative measures. If we are to reduce the amount of money spent on hospital care, and on doctor-related clinic visits, then we have to move to prevent the illness or physical injury in the first place. Working with the public school system on nutritional awareness and fitness is an important component of these preventive measures, as is the development of workplace standards.

The government did introduce new guidelines for employers in the workplace. This new approach to workplace design and permitted employee activity is called ergonomics. Ergonomic procedures have been implemented for years in countries like Germany and Japan, in different models. In the new ergonomics handbook published by the government in 1994, there are numerous new standards for the physical work environment, such as the height of desks, the amount of turning that an employee may do, the maximum weight that an employee may lift, and so on. Nowhere, however, is there any discussion of general health measures that an employee should follow. If it is the role of the employer to maintain a healthy workplace, then it surely is the role of the employee to keep herself or himself healthy in order to be fit for work.

So too with health care in general. The Seaton Commission pointed out quite correctly that there must be much more education provided children by their parents regarding the general parameters of a healthy lifestyle. We must help Generation "R" to stop smoking, to reduce alcohol consumption, and to get into an active program of physical fitness with a properly regulated diet.

The approach to health care taken by the Progressive Democratic Alliance is an holistic one that places the first priority on prevention. It is our view that a multi-tiered system of services must be established ranging from diagnostic and treatment clinics up to full research hospitals. With our population aging and the demand for health services rising, there is a need to re-focus our view of our health care system. The fact that we enjoy a comprehensive, portable, accessible, and affordable health care system is part of what Canada is all about. If we are to protect Medicare, then we must put a more progressive plan in place that recognizes our changing demographic patterns.

HOSPITAL AND HEALTH CARE REGIONS

The Progressive Democratic Alliance believes that change within the system to facilitate better health care delivery will only happen when we re-examine the concept of Regional Hospitals, and make provision to get doctors, both general practitioners and specialists, out of the urban centres and into our hinterland. What we propose is the establishment of an hierarchical system of facilities through which the individual's medical requirements will be met according to his or her special needs. Non-emergency patients would proceed, as necessary, through the following treatment tiers:

1) the doctor's office,

2) local diagnostic and treatment clinics,

3) community hospitals able to refer patients in need of specialists to

4) regional hospitals—one per region—that will be served by

5) the full research and medical facilities of the large urban hospitals that, in turn, will have the benefit of

6) expanded research laboratory facilities to tackle the more complex medical research needs that will be undertaken in conjunction with the major universities within the province.

Certainly, all communities should be served by clinics that have both diagnostic and treatment facilities, although this has not been the pattern to date within the province. The adequate funding of these clinics would take considerable pressure off community hospitals, and reduce the direct cost of the service. Similarly, the development of adequately funded regional hospitals will encourage physicians, especially specialists, to take their practice to these interior centres, where, given the current medical billing practice, there is little at present to attract them. Therefore, it is important for government to provide the proper facilities, and to put in place regulations that will increase the opportunities for new graduates and for foreign specialists who come to Canada.

No doubt there will be some argument between communities as to where Regional Hospitals should be established, especially in areas like the Kootenays, where the aging Trail Hospital has functioned as a regional centre for many years. A good argument, for example, could be made for building any new Regional Hospital in Cranbrook. Clearly, the final decision would rest with representatives of all the residents within the health region (such as those elected to the regional Health Board) and those from the funding agency, which is the provincial government. Whatever the case, if we are to meet the needs of the people who, in increasing numbers, are living outside the Lower Mainland, there is a real need to establish regional medical centres throughout the province.

LIMITING BILLING NUMBERS

In addition, the British Columbia Medical Association, in its contract with the government, will have to agree to limit the billing numbers granted to newly licensed doctors, unless they are prepared to locate their practices outside the Lower Mainland. Similarly, as mentioned earlier, the current practice of limiting the placement and restricting the tenure of foreign physicians must be changed, if we are to reverse the adverse effects of qualified BC medical specialists moving to the United States. In the final analysis, of course, success is dependent on putting in place a long-range plan to provide the best possible facilities in our regional hospitals.

A FINAL WORD

As elsewhere noted, the comprehensive, portable, accessible and affordable health care system we enjoy is part of what Canada is all about. If we are to protect Medicare, then we must put a more progressive Health Plan in place that recognizes the changing patterns of population growth and accommodates the resultant increased demands. The approach to health care taken by the Progressive Democratic Alliance is one that encompasses all the necessary changes, but places the first priority on prevention.

SURVIVING CONFEDERATION:

A BACKUP PLAN FOR BRITISH COLUMBIA

CANADA AND THE QUEBEC QUESTION: TRUDEAU

In early 1992, I journeyed to Montreal to meet with Pierre Trudeau and Quebec Premier Robert Bourassa to better my understanding of Quebec's position in what was then the latest round in Canada's constitutional debate. My first appointment was with Trudeau, who had invited me to meet him for lunch at the historic Mount Royal Club, which I considered a particular honour. We had not met privately before, although we had corresponded over a number of years on such matters as the fight for a "Just Society" in Canada, the function of a strong central government, and the general state of politics across our country. To a degree, my success in the 1991 provincial election was the pass that now helped me past the door with the former Canadian

Prime Minister, who confessed a keenness to hear how I had managed to take the Liberal Party from relative obscurity to the status of Opposition in a province where polarized politics had been the order of the day for half a century.

What I thought would be a brief luncheon turned into a two-and-a-half-hour meeting, and will be remembered by me as one of the most stimulating of my life, as the former Prime Minister gave me his thoughts on the "Quebec Question", and much more. The one point that Trudeau made particularly clear to me was that if we allowed the provinces to become too powerful there would be little left of the Canada we had come to know and love. I was surprised at his confidence in the intelligence of the Canadian people to make the right decision in this, because he had long been portrayed in the media as an arrogant, aloof man, who held his fellow citizens in contempt. Canadians, he told me, are a fair and just people who can be trusted to stand up for their country when called upon to do so, but they required continued leadership and direction to counter that other threat to our national existence: the continental economic forces that had coopted the Mulroney government and temporarily beguiled the Canadian electorate in 1988. If we were not careful, they too would destroy us.

We talked at length about the Free Trade Agreement, and the propaganda process employed by Mulroney and his Free Trade cohorts to soften Canadian public opinion towards economic "harmonization" (integration) with the United States. There was an energy in his intensely blue eyes, when Trudeau defended his introduction of the

Foreign Investment Review Agency and the National Energy Program, both of which, he argued, had been intended to secure Canadians ownership of their own economy, and thus their independence as a nation state. What was more, only the economic security of our people could cure our continuing constitutional crises. "It is hard," he said, "to be charitable toward your neighbour, when you can't make ends meet yourself."

My discussion with Trudeau brought to mind a lesson I had learned in my last year as an undergraduate, when I spent some time in a Buddhist monastery in Japan. There, the elderly monk who had been assigned my welfare (probably as a penance) instructed me not to trust that which we sense only with our eyes, but to trust instead that which we feel when our eyes provide vision to the soul. He told me that we must focus on that which touches all our senses and not merely one of them. "When you point a finger toward the moon," he said, "be sure that you see the moon, and not the finger." Too often in Canada, as Trudeau so eloquently argued that stormy winter's afternoon, we do not have a vision of our nation, but see only various of its component parts. We are focused on the finger and cannot see the moon.

All over the world, people are knocking down the walls that divide them, both literally and figuratively. When the Berlin wall crumbled, the world celebrated the end of the Soviet empire and the Cold War. When Nelson Mandela finally broke through the historic wall of discrimination to bring equal rights to the black majority in South Africa, the world rejoiced. In Canada, however, we have become so pre-occupied with questions related to amending our Constitution to include special references to the inalienable rights and privileges of the Quebecois and Aboriginal peoples (not to mention those of social minorities such as homosexuals) that we have somehow forgotten that they are but parts of the larger entity. And while we labour on barriers to divide us, American financial interests pick off our resource and other industries like some uninvited guest at a Sunday smorgasbord. Indeed, I wonder if in ten years people will ask themselves whatever happened to the fantastic country that once spanned the northern portion of continental North America.

CANADA AND THE QUEBEC QUESTION: BOURASSA

When, later that day, I met with Premier Bourassa in his Montreal office, he told me in the frankest of terms that it was only a matter of time before Canada became a collection of semi-independent states caught up in the vortex of the American economy. His primary concern was *not* the survival of Canada in this context, but the preservation of French Canada—something that could only be achieved by assuring the supremacy of the French language, customs, and system of law within the political boundaries of the province of Quebec. That is to say, the first concern of the Premier was to continue to construct walls around the French language and culture to prevent their erosion.

As I listened to Bourassa, I could not help but be

reminded of the story of King Canute, who demonstrated the limits of his powers for all to see by ordering back the incoming tide. Bourassa felt that without special guarantees within Confederation (or, failing this, sovereignty), Quebec would find it impossible to prevail as a French enclave in an English-speaking North American sea. It was this fear of the inevitable that led him in 1974 to enact Bill 98, the first of his province's laws to protect the French language, legislation which was extended and strengthened by René Levesque's infamous Bill 101 in 1977. Canadians from coast to coast protested to no avail against these clearly discriminatory measures.

Like many of my fellow citizens, I firmly believe that the retention of one's language and culture is important, but I do not believe that they can be protected long through legislation. Neither do I feel that it is acceptable to discriminate against minorities, and especially not for the purpose of maintaining the dominance of a cultural majority. In simple terms: merchants should be able to put up signs outside their stores in the languages of their choice. The state should not hold the power to prohibit this most basic level of freedom of expression—a judgement that has been confirmed by the United Nations Human Rights Commission.

Premier Bourassa had supported the 1987 Meech Lake Agreement (which was defeated by a single vote in the Manitoba Legislature) because it contained provisions that would have recognized Quebec as a "distinct society", and would have undone the constitutional amending formula of 1982 (which had taken fifty years to achieve) to restore Quebec's veto power over all future changes to the Canadian Constitution. The Premier told me he felt this would have been a small price to pay to keep Canada together. Bourassa, of course, believed in the compact theory of the Canadian confederation. Somewhat ironically, I thought, he saw the United States as an ally to his cause because it provided such a huge market for Quebec's hydro-electric power, and was such an important source of investment capital for Quebec's mining and forest industries in the area north of the settlements along the narrow flood plain of the lower St. Lawrence River.

At one point, Bourassa asked me what it was that I thought English Canada wanted. I tried hard to explain that I could not give him a definitive answer because, if we took Main Street in Vancouver as a microcosm, we could see a nation made up of many cultures, from every possible region of the globe. These people, who had immigrated to Canada for reasons not dissimilar to those of the earlier French and British settlers, may have learned how to speak English, but that didn't make them *English* Canadians in any racial sense. Consequently, although Canada had within its history the division between two nations, British and French, it was no longer centred on this division. And that Canada's uniqueness now lies in its celebration of the differences between its peoples, all of whom have come together to live in peace with dignity.

Of course, it is also true that Quebec has a sizeable minority of people for whom French is not their first language, and for whom French ancestry is not a functional part of their heritage. Their rights have to be protected as well, if they are to enjoy, as they must, equal opportunity with their French-speaking counterparts. Furthermore, even if every immigrant to Quebec were French-speaking, it does not mean that these people somehow have any cultural links to the Quebecois. When I put these points to Mr. Bourassa, he replied by patiently describing his government's strategy for achieving a yet another "new arrangement with Ottawa", one that Mr. Trudeau, only hours earlier, had predicted would defeat the Quebec Liberals at the next provincial election and bring the Parti Quebecois back to power.

The essence of Bourassa's proposed "new" arrangement with Ottawa was essentially Meech Lake all over again. It called for greater powers for the province of Quebec, including a veto over future constitutional changes, control over immigration, control over the delivery of federal programs such as employment training and arts funding, and, of course, recognition of Quebec as a distinct society. This was the minimum Bourassa thought he needed to satisfy the increasing demands made upon him by those within his own party who wished to have more authority within an increasingly sovereign Quebec, as well as to save his own political future. To that end, he set an autumn 1992 deadline on achieving a new constitutional accord with Ottawa, or he would hold a referendum within his province on Quebec's future.

In the event, all Canadians went to the polls that October 26th in a referendum on the Charlottetown Accord, which contained Bourassa's constitutional wish list and much more, and voted to reject it by a margin of 54.4 percent. On a province-by-province basis, it was defeated in Nova Scotia, Manitoba, Saskatchewan, Alberta, and British Columbia because it was ill-considered, vague, confusing, over-sold, and seemed to offer Quebec too much; in Quebec it was defeated because it was ill-considered, vague, confusing, over-sold, and didn't seem to offer Quebec enough—"mere tokenism" the separatists cried. Bourassa would retire before the next provincial election in Quebec, but Trudeau's prediction proved correct: the Parti Quebecois emerged triumphant in 1994. And we began to dance to the "Constitutional Rag" all over again!

HISTORICAL PERSPECTIVE

Of course, the "two founding nations" view of Confederation held by Premier Bourassa and many others in Quebec, perhaps even a majority, was not without some historical justification. Quebec's cultural distinctiveness within the British Empire had been guaranteed by the Quebec Act of 1774. The arrival, after the American Revolution, of the displaced United Empire Loyalists from Britain's former thirteen colonies did not change this in any fundamental way. The Constitutional Act of 1791 may have given some of the Quebecois their first taste of representative government, but it divided the Canadian colony into a predominantly French-speaking and still largely culturally distinct Lower Canada (Quebec), and an English-speaking Upper Canada (Ontario), where British institutions and practices prevailed.

It was the Act of Union in 1841, however, which followed in the wake of the Durham Report on the Canadian Rebellions of 1837-38, that has given the compact theory of confederation such legitimacy as it has ever had.

Under this constitutional arrangement, which ignored democratic considerations of representation by population, the two Canadas (Quebec and Ontario) were united as equal territorial partners in what amounted to a semi-federated state. The British North America Act of 1867 ended this ultimately unworkable experiment to create a federal union of Quebec, Ontario, Nova Scotia, and New Brunswick, the terms and conditions of which had been negotiated and agreed to by most of the leading colonial politicians of the day, both French and English.

This new Canadian constitution guaranteed—as it continues to do—the Quebecois their language, their Napoleonic civil code, their Roman Catholic educational institutions, the very broad provincial authority that would be judicially interpreted as having been conferred upon their provincial government under the "property and civil rights" provision of the BNA Act's Section 92, provincial control over local government, as well as such representation in the Parliament of Canada as to virtually guarantee that no national government could ever be formed without their active participation. Of course, in that Canada was still a British colony in 1867, and the BNA Act an act of the Parliament at Westminster, constitutional vetos for any of the Canadian provinces were not at issue. These decisions, when necessary, would be rendered until 1949 by the

Judicial Committee of the Imperial Privy Council.

So although there clearly is a foundation within the fundamental law of Canada in support of the "two founding nations" concept of Confederation, such argument conveniently substitutes Ottawa for Ontario in its partnership with Quebec, and ignores the consequences of the transcontinental, nation-building exercise that began in 1867 with the expansion of the 1841 Ontario-Quebec union to include the self-governing colonies Nova Scotia and New Brunswick. Nor does it consider the acquisition of the Hudson Bay territories and the creation of Manitoba in 1870, the negotiated entry into confederation of the additional self-governing colonies of British Columbia in 1871 and Prince Edward Island in 1873, the creation of Saskatchewan and Alberta in 1905, and the constitutional terms of Newfoundland's entry into the Canadian confederation in 1949. In fact, it ignores one hundred and thirty years of history: of participation in two world wars, of industrialization, of changing demographics, of creating national transportation and communications systems, of a developing national social contract, and of taking our independent place on the world stage—of evolution from colony to nation state, one and indivisible from sea unto sea unto sea.

THE 1995 QUEBEC REFERENDUM

Canadians, however, need to reflect long and hard on the result of the 30 October 1995 Quebec referendum on whether to separate from Canada or not. The final tally of "Yes" and

"No" ballots gave those on the "No" side the slimmest of majorities—51.4% to 49.6%. So slim, that there really was no victor. There was, however, a big loser, and that was Canada! As I watched the returns come in, two things struck me. First, if it were not for the "Anglophone" and "Alophone" (read "English" and "Ethnic" Canadian) vote in Montreal, the "Yes" side would have won. Second, any pretense that what is going on in Quebec is other than the protection of the white Francophone race, vanished with the speech of Premier Parizeau after the final count was in. What I found ironic was the horrified reaction of political leaders in the rest of the country to the Premier's racist comments. Where had these people been? What did they think that the Quebecois meant when they said they are a "distinct society"? Do they really believe that the drive toward separatism in Quebec is designed merely to promote a sort of renewed federalism in the province and, in result, throughout the rest of the country?

CONTEMPORARY CANADA

We are living in an age of political correctness where certain subjects have been placed on the taboo list. When, for example, one asks how it is possible to have as Her Majesty's Loyal Opposition in the Parliament of Canada a party that ran candidates in only one of the ten provinces, captured less than fifteen percent of the national vote, and has as its raison d'être the breakup of our nation, we are admonished in hushed tones, because the party in question happens to come from the province of Quebec. If we speak out, then we lack sensitivity toward the people of Quebec, or worse, we are anti-French!

It is time to end the masquerade and get down to basics. The "federal" Bloc Quebecois and the provincial Parti Quebecois want to create a separate country in Quebec, in which the white Francophone population is guaranteed its majority status in perpetuity. These separatists have no interest in the devolution of federal powers to the provinces, constitutional reform, or even sovereignty association. They want independence, and nothing less.

The proof of this, if further proof were needed, is that the distinctive character of Quebec is already recognized across our land and, as shown above, more than adequately protected in the Canadian constitution. What is more, the 1982 Canada Act, which patriated our constitution from Britain and gave Canadians their Charter of Rights, provides a "notwithstanding" clause that allows Quebec to avoid challenges to such of its legislation that impinges on the basic liberties of its minority citizens. In addition, the province can opt out of national programs when it deems that these do not serve its particular interests; or it can negotiate special agreements with Ottawa, as it has done on taxation and immigration. In short, Quebec's argument with the rest of Canada cannot be about the devolution of powers from Ottawa (as the Canadian corporate media and our federal politicians would have had us believe during the Charlottetown Accord debate), because they already have all the power they need to protect whatever they decide the distinctive character of their province entails.

CHRETIEN'S BLUNDER

The legislation introduced by Prime Minister Jean Chretien in February of 1996 to give Quebec, Ontario, the Atlantic Provinces, the West, and British Columbia constitutional vetoes means that future constitutional change in Canada will be impossible if it is not agreeable to Quebec. Further, Chretien's decision to provide Quebec "distinct society" status (however this is finally worded) can only serve to encourage it to abandon all hesitation in abrogating minority rights when the interests of the Francophone majority so demand.

What we saw in the last weeks of the 1995 referendum campaign, when finally he awakened to the fact that the "No" forces that supported Canadian federalism were about to lose the vote, was a shaken and rather frightened Prime Minister. In desperation, he promised to give Quebec that which the Canadian people had expressly rejected in 1992. Even if these provisions to recognize Quebec as a distinct society and provide it a veto are but a guide to Parliament, and not formal constitutional amendments, they fly directly in the face of the wishes of the Canadian people who have made quite clear their support for a strong national government and ten equal provinces.

Although I can't imagine what it might be, one must assume that there must have been some calculation of clear political gain for himself and his party for the Prime Minister to have taken this course. Thus far, his view that Canada is made up of two founding peoples and five regions has not sat well with Canadians in general, and especially not with those in BC, whose "region" was included as an afterthought. Besides, it is an old concept, one that has been rejected before, and will not sell now.

Chretien's "five region" approach fits the "heartland and hinterland" model, which defines the "real" Canada as its industrial heartland—the corridor from Windsor to Quebec City, in which most Canadians live. The rest of us live in the hinterland, where our role is to supply raw materials to the heartland. This is a vision of Canada that in the past has begat Western alienation, and the Prime Minister made a real blunder by reintroducing it, if only because it serves to remind those who live outside Central Canada that our federal parliamentary structure does not serve well the interests of provinces other than Ontario and Quebec.

Very little changed with the election of Jean Chretien and the federal Liberals in 1993. His distinct society and veto policies will do nothing to change the demands of Quebec. They will, however, render fruitless any attempt at meaningful constitutional change in Canada as a whole. Meanwhile, Chretien continues the real negotiations with the province of Quebec, wherein resides his political future. The realpolitik in Canada is that, in most federal elections, Quebecois voters have decided which party forms the government.

One has only to ask, for example, why there is really no debate in the House of Commons about the fitness of the

Bloc Quebecois to hold the status of Official Opposition. To my mind, the one reason why its activities are not considered seditious is that the Prime Minister also believes that this country is made up of two nations, and that the Bloc are legitimate representives of the Quebec people. I have seen absolutely no evidence to the contrary. Indeed, there is mounting evidence to suggest that the largesse that the federal government continues to shower on the province of Quebec will actually increase as a result of the closeness of the 1995 referendum vote.

TWO OPTIONS FOR CANADA

Historically, Canada was built in defiance of continental forces that sought to divide us, and through that division erode our commitment to the continuance of our nation. Unfortunately, over the last decade, the trade and tariff barriers, foreign ownership restrictions, and social and cultural institutions which previously had protected Canada have come down or have been significantly weakened. This has left us vulnerable to those American interests that seek to control our economy (including control over our so-called cultural industries), and to reduce us to the level of their domestic playing field by destroying our medicare, unemployment benefits, and Canada Pension Plan. Of course, Canadians are the authors of their own destiny in this regard, in that the political will to go along with these American influences was never higher than during the Mulroney years from 1984 to 1993.

One might have expected Chretien to attempt to reverse the trend, but there doesn't seem to be any plan to do anything of the kind. When I read a federal budget that is written more for the American investment community than for the Canadian people, I am alarmed. When I see this nation being carved up, and its railways, airlines—perhaps even parts of its public broadcasting corporation—sold off to appease foreigners, I am angry. When I see Canadian farmers, fishers, foresters, miners, small business entrepreneurs, teachers, mill workers, health care providers, homemakers, our youth and seniors sold out, all in the name of some economic master plan, I am resolved to do something about it. So what are our options?

In my view, Canada has only two options: (1) either we continue down the path we are on, which will lead to every province acting strictly for itself with no commitments to national standards or programs—an approach that will greatly speed up our absorption into whatever the United States decides finally to make of us; or (2) we seek to create a new federal system of equal provinces, with a strong central government dedicated to maintaining national standards in health care, education, and social services, while holding the forces of continentalism and Quebec separatism at bay.

Obviously, the first option leaves me cold. As to the second, I think the Premier of British Columbia should send a clear message to Ottawa and to the other provincial capitals demanding that we immediately start working toward the creation of a renewed Canada. This, of course, will require a measure of leadership we heretofore have not seen from the office of the Premier. When Lucien Bouchard visited Victoria in 1994 in his then role as Leader of Her Majesty's *Loyal* Opposition in Ottawa to promote the separation of his home province from Canada, Premier Harcourt's response in such debate as took place in the BC Legislature was pathetic. Indeed, discussion of BC's options in all of this continues to be discouraged by most provincial politicians. Perhaps the new Premier will rise to this challenge. If he does, and should intransigence prevail on the part of our partners in Confederation, British Columbia, at least, has a third option.

A THIRD OPTION FOR BRITISH COLUMBIA

We can go it alone! On the occasion of the 1994 Bouchard visit, I released a statement that suggested that if Quebec was given the freedom to separate, BC should consider its options within the remaining Confederation. To say that there was public interest in my suggestion is to understate the response. In fact, it was overwhelming, as British Columbians wrote, phoned, and faxed their agreement. I believe that British Columbians should be prepared for whatever occurs. The only thing that will set this province back in the event of Quebec's successful separation from Canada will be if we have no plan to deal with the consequences.

It would be wrong to imply that even a substantial minority of British Columbians are raging separatists, because they are not. The majority of British Columbians are as dedicated as any of their fellow Canadians to building a strong nation, but a mood of deep resentment has developed within their province over the last two decades of the ongoing constitutional debate in response to the arrogant views so often expressed by people who live in Central Canada, and to what they regard as a lack of direction and leadership on national issues. What may have begun as a feeling of uncertainty has turned to alienation and even fear as a result of the 1995 referendum in Quebec.

The very idea that one province, by simple majority vote, can tear this country of 30 million people asunder is offensive to a large number of British Columbians. The fact that no federal politician has taken the position that Quebec cannot withdraw from our Confederation on this basis confounds the intelligent mind. Let us imagine that, with a good turn out at the polls in the next referendum in 1997, seventy percent of the roughly 5 million eligible voters cast their ballots, and of that number 50 percent plus one vote to separate. Then, in effect, some 1.75 million people—less than 6 percent of all Canadians—will have decided our fate. Nor is there consolation in the suggestion advanced by a number of prominent Canadians that in the event of a vote to separate, Quebec itself will be divided, unless, of course, one can look with equanimity on complete social breakdown and civil strife.

Nevertheless, British Columbians look on in disbelief as our tax dollars are spent in ever-increasing amounts in an attempt to influence what will be a negotiated separation of Quebec, and a dramatic, non-democratic breakup of Canada. Federal Liberal politicians bristle at the suggestion that they are involved in negotiating this breakup. Before the 1995 referendum, they argued that their very silence on the question of Quebec separation had removed them from the heat of the provincial debate, and that this was having a positive effect on popular support for the federal option in Quebec. Given the actual result of the referendum, the very fact that this argument was ever seriously put forward should set off alarm bells in BC. It represented the complete lack of political will on the part of the Chretien government to pre-empt the possible breakup of Canada by putting before the Canadian people a renewed vision of their Nation. There are no federal politicians prepared to advance a vision of a strong central government with ten strong and *equal* partners in one united and indivisible country called Canada, which might then include recognition of the distinctiveness of both the Quebecois and Aboriginal peoples in a context of equality in law.

Our country is at the crossroads. Unfortunately, the path that seems most appealing to Chretien is to yield to Quebec on the questions of constitutional veto, "distinct society", and the transfer of federal powers. The federal Liberals conveniently forget that British Columbians roundly rejected the Charlottetown Accord, which contained the very provisions that Chretien is now putting in place. This too should set off alarm bells in British Columbia.

There are many reasons why British Columbians have a right to feel shortchanged by the current federal government's political agenda. The federal government's cancellation of KAON and diversion of the icebreaker contract to Quebec are both examples of the disdain with which British Columbians are treated in Ottawa. The closure of the Armed Forces base at Chilliwack is another. So too are the cutbacks in transfer payments from the federal government.

THE PROGRESSIVE DEMOCRATIC ALLIANCE

The PDA is committed to the position that I took during the debates over the Meech Lake Agreement in 1987 and the Charlottetown Accord in 1992 that the first priority of British Columbians must be that BC is an equal partner in a strong and united Canada. We are committed to Canadian federalism as the first priority, but to British Columbia in the final analysis. In order to fulfil this latter commitment, we believe that BC must have a plan in place that will protect the interests of its residents should the federal government fail to do so.

ASSESSING THE VIABILITY OF AN INDEPENDENT BRITISH COLUMBIA

To seriously discuss the independence of British Columbia, we must canvass the following issues: (1) What will be the territory of this new nation state? (2) Can BC stand alone in terms of its economy? (3) What about currency? (4) What about citizenship? (5) Will BC be a sovereign state, but associated with Canada? (6) Would we be better off convincing

Alberta to come with us? All of these questions are legitimate, and need to be fully examined. Let me then remove my politician's hat to put on my professional hat as an economic geographer and try objectively to assess BC's chances of going it alone.

TERRITORY AND ECONOMY

In terms of territory, British Columbia's 947,800 square kilometres represent about 10% of the total area of Canada. Roughly 929,703 sq. km of BC is land; the remaining 18,100 sq. km is fresh water. Thus, BC has an abundance of water for domestic consumption, irrigation, industrial use, as well as for hydro-electric production which accounts for over 70 billion megawatt hours annually. It also has a rich primary resource base, much of which is renewable. What is more, BC is rich in the most important of resources: an educated and mobile workforce. There is no reason why BC's territorial base should change by so much as one square kilometer.

British Columbia enjoys one of the strongest economies, measured on a per capita basis, in Canada, with a annual GDP of approximately $87 billion, and a per capita GDP of $26,900—roughly the same as Ontario, and second only to Alberta, where per capita GDP exceeds $28,600. A total of $32 billion dollars is generated annually in British Columbia from forestry and forest product manufacturing alone, which is almost 38% of the national total. Although the 1995 resource revenue projection from mining was less than one billion dollars (due to restrictive government policy), in 1993 it was $2.8 billion. In addition, over $1.5 billion was generated from farm gate receipts in agriculture. Merchandising in BC's automotive industry accounted for over $6.7 billion in 1993, with the food industry not far behind at $6.2 billion.

By virtue of the natural valley corridors that run north/ south, British Columbia has ready access to the American markets to its south. It also has a long and relatively accessible coast line of 17,856 km, with two established ports on the mainland, Vancouver and Prince Rupert, and two accessible ports on Vancouver Island, Victoria and Port Alberni. Well situated on the Pacific Rim, it has excellent potential for expanded trade with the rapidly developing economies of India, Vietnam, and Indochina, as well as with the established economies of Japan, China, Taiwan, and Korea. An added advantage exists in the fact that Vancouver and Prince Rupert are the only port facilities through which the provinces of Alberta, Saskatchewan, and Manitoba can access Asian markets on a cost-effective basis. In short, we have a solid economy upon which to build a satisfying, comfortable, *limits-to-growth* future appropriate to the demands and limitations of the 21st century.

AN ADDENDUM: GOVERNMENT DEBT

The only serious economic crunch that we have in British Columbia is the size of our provincial debt and our share of the Canadian national debt. Our provincial debt in 1995/96 is anticipated to rise to almost $28 billion dollars, with an annual borrowing cost of about $1.7 billion. Keep in mind that we have only 3.3 million people, and that our population projections remain modest due to the fourth lowest birth rate in the country and, for the moment at least, a restrictive policy on immigration. Of the total $28 billion provincial debt, almost 10.2 billion is in direct government spending, with the balance, about $17.8 billion, carried in loans for capital construction and crown corporations.

The thorny problem that will confront us should Quebec leave Confederation is the division of responsibility for the remaining national debt. For example, how much of our present provincial debt was caused by the federal government's arbitrary cuts in its support for those programs for which it has a legal financial obligation. British Columbia would argue that it has a credit position with the federal government because it has suffered a per capita reduction beyond those of any other province in federal transfers for such programs as the Canada Assistance Program. Of course, if there is no federal government left with which to negotiate, this won't make much difference. It will simply be a question of how much of the $700 billion national debt is BC's share, and how much belongs to the other provinces and territories, whatever their political configuration in the rest of Canada. There are no easy answers, yet we are in a better position than any other province because of our history as a "have" province, and our long record of tax-dollar transfers to Ottawa. Consequently, I am still optimistic about our economic future.

A CURRENCY OF OUR OWN

Should this province decide to take the bold step of separating from the rest of Canada after Quebec leaves Confederation, the question of what currency we use thereafter will quickly arise. Will British Columbia have to launch its own currency? The short answer is probably, yes. It is inconceivable to me that we could then entertain sharing the same currency, if the monetary policy governing Canadian currency continued to be set in Ottawa. I realize that there has been a great deal of discussion about the employment of the Canadian dollar in a separate Quebec, but I find the argument of the Quebec separatists that somehow they will have representation on the Board of the Bank of Canada, and thus exercise influence over monetary policy appropriate to the needs of a sovereign state, patently absurd.

So, how would a British Columbian currency fare? The answer is that our BC dollar would fare quite well. Although it is true that international credit rating agencies are keeping a watchful eye on BC's debt-to-population ratio, our provincial credit rating in 1995 was good, and it will continue to be so, even when we assume our share of the federal debt. What is more, the implementation of the package of economic, social, administrative, and taxation reforms advocated by the Progressive Democratic Alliance, which anticipate the emergence of a new global village, would make BC's currency among the world's most stable as we enter the 21st century.

CONSIDERATIONS AND DANGERS

What about citizenship? Will BC be a sovereign state, but associated with Canada? Would we be better off convincing Alberta to come with us? Of course, a sovereign British Columbia would have its own citizenship and passports. As to the nature of any future association with Canada, or Alberta, this depends on the eventual political configuration of the rest of Canada. Could Ontario hold the Prairies, the Atlantic provinces, and the Territories together as a country? Probably it could not. What then? The answer is that no one knows for sure.

One must assume, however, that the continentalist forces to the south would be quick to move in with a view to establishing the political and economic integration of the Canadian provinces and territories, British Columbia included. This thought may not be a crazy as one might first think. The United States covets our water resources, and would like nothing better than to have access to our huge resource base, particularly in light of the new conservation measures that are in place south of the border governing forestry, fishing, and mining. Besides, BC is America's land bridge to Alaska.

PUBLIC DEBATE

However horrible the prospect, British Columbians must begin a public debate on the merits of some plan of action to protect themselves if there is no national leadership to keep this country together. On the face of it, British Columbia would do quite well as a small nation state. BC's separation from Canada, as unthinkable as that is for us all, may well be the only way we have to protect the quality of life that we have learned to love as members of Canadian society. It will be ironic indeed if our only chance to save the Canadian way of life is to leave Canada. What is at stake are medicare, quality public education, and a progressive social safety net—Canadian institutions that respect the fundamental rights and equality of each of our citizens—as well as a solid, free enterprise economy accessed and owned by Canadians.

FIGHTING FOR CANADA

> As a Canadian living in British Columbia, I am committed to the fight to keep Canada together.

> But let there be no mistake, it is the Canadian ideal, the just society, that I struggle for.

> And if this can no longer be found in my country, then I will fight to protect it in my province.

> And I will fight for my province to stand alone in the world, if need be, to achieve this.

> To paraphrase Pierre Elliot Trudeau: if we are going to destroy Canada, let's do it with a bang, not a whimper.

> If we are not, then let's stand up and fight for our country!

WHERE PHILOSOPHIES AND CULTURES COLLIDE:

THE ABORIGINAL LAND QUESTION

THE CHARLOTTETOWN ACCORD

The small room was filled with people seated on narrow wooden chairs that had been placed in rows by the party faithful. This townhall meeting in Quesnel was one in a series organized in 1992 by the BC Liberal Party to discuss the proposed changes to the Canadian constitution contained in the Charlottetown Accord. My speech provided the audience an outline of the Accord and its provision for the three "Canadas", which it described as "French Canada," "Aboriginal Canada", and the "Rest of Canada (ROC)". In attendance were two young, well dressed, aboriginal women. From their neutral body language it was difficult to determine what they thought of what I was saying about the Aboriginal Package contained in the Accord.

During the question and answer session that followed, the inevitable was asked about land claims, and the implications of the Accord's proposal that defined Aboriginal self-government as independence from provincial and federal statutes. I gave the same answer that I have always given. I do not favour the creation of an order of government that would give jurisdiction over land where special rights, special privilege and status would be entrenched on the basis of an individual's racial origin.

To my mind, the foundation of a democratic society rests on the fundamental principle of equality. We cannot be equal if there are lines, either tangible or invisible, that divide people or discriminate against one person over another. Having grown up in a colonial state in Africa, where there was open discrimination based on one's race, not only between black and white, but between the different African tribes and between African and Asian, I cannot accept that we should enjoin constitutional reform that entrenches such distinctions.

In particular, I did not favour the proposal that was in the Accord because it entrenched the worst of the Indian Act, first proclaimed in 1876, into modern constitutional law. In other words, the basic tenet within the proposed Charlottetown Accord was that the "status" of Indian that our forefathers stamped on the foreheads of people who were racially North American would translate into a form of "citizenship" that would carry with it exclusive rights to land, resources, and governance. But there was no description of how this form of Aboriginal self-government would work, except that its structure would be whatever the First Nations employed prior to European settlement.

Fair enough, but what obligations will the federal or provincial government have with respect to the protection of *individual* rights of Aboriginal people who may not wish to be governed by a tribal collective Chief and Council model. My concern was, and is, that the discriminatory powers of the State, well practiced under the Indian Act, may well be transferred directly to a new set of elites within the Aboriginal community. If that is done under the guise of Aboriginal self-government, what protection will those governed by this new elite have should discriminatory practice continue. This is especially true for women and children within those Indian Bands that reject the principles of individual rights spelled out within the Canadian Charter of Rights and Freedoms.

My response to the questions regarding the cost of Aboriginal self-government was simple: neither the federal nor the provincial governments can afford what will be demanded, so why carry on a charade that will entrench special rights and privileges, already seen to be discriminatory within the existing Indian Act, at a price that is well beyond the means of the Canadian taxpayer? The real question surrounding the existing rights and jurisdictions of the Aboriginal people in BC, given the absence of treaties, is whether or not the aboriginal people ever sanctioned the transfer of land and authority to the British Crown, and the only venue to hear that argument is the Supreme Court of Canada. Whatever the outcome, I told the meeting, we must establish that every Canadian is equal to every other Canadian regardless of race, colour, creed, language, religion, or gender.

ABORIGINAL PERSPECTIVES

It was at this point that one of the two young Aboriginal women rose to her feet, and spoke with a quiet firmness. At first she spoke in her native tongue, perhaps to impress upon the crowd her distinctive cultural background. She introduced us to the name of "her people", and gave a short history of their evolution in the Cariboo. She then turned and asked me a very powerful question: "Do you, Mr. Wilson, think that you have an equal right to this land as I do? Do you really think that you are my equal?"

I responded in the affirmative: "Yes. I respect the fact that we may all originate from different backgrounds, that we may speak a different mother tongue, practice a different religion, but we should, all of us, be equal under the civil and criminal code. Equality under the law is imperative. Just because we are different does not mean that we are not equal."

To that she politely but firmly responded that Canadian law holds nothing for her people. She cited a long litany of abuses that had been directed against her people, abuses she claimed originated at the hands of early settlers, the Church, government, and, most recently, the RCMP and the Canadian justice system. She told the gathered crowd in a most passionate way that I was in fact not her equal because I was not one of her people, I was an "alien". I had, she said,

111

stolen the land from her people, and I was responsible for the repression of her people. She continued by saying that while all Canadians may be equal, she was not Canadian, she was a First Nations citizen, and would fight for her right to remain so.

All this she said without raising her voice, and the message obviously came from her heart. She firmly believed that she and her companion were not, nor would they ever be, Canadians, and she held equally firmly the belief that the Aboriginal and the non-Aboriginal communities were irrevocably separated by race, and that was the way they wished it to be. Listening to her, and watching her intensity, I found it hard not to feel sympathy for her argument, and I had difficulty for a moment staying focused on the principle and philosophy that have become so much a part of me.

"What you say is interesting," I commented, "but it makes me wonder why you are here. Will you vote in the next election?"

"Yes," she answered.

"Would I be given an equal opportunity to vote in an election for your government?" I asked.

"No," was her curt reply.

The double standard was there for all to see, but that did not alter her view. Neither did the fact that the leadership of her "people" had made it clear that the Canadian Charter provisions of equality would not be accepted in the governance of her community. It made me wonder how she might prevail in a society where men and women were not treated equally. I further wondered how the obvious divisions of opinion within Aboriginal society with respect to how they should approach constitutional reform will be dealt with through their own political structures.

On another occasion, I was in the cafe of a sturdy little ferry, the Queen of Chilliwack, crossing a stormy Jervis Inlet from Earls Cove to Saltery Bay, en route to Powell River, when an elderly Aboriginal woman came up to my table and sat down. "I seen ya on TV. You that Wilson fella aren't ya?" I smilingly replied that I was. "Why do you hate my people?" she asked, rocking me to my core. "I don't hate your people. Why would you say that?" "I seen ya on TV, " she said. "You're against the land claim."

What followed was one of the most moving conversations I have experienced. A more gentle, sensitive individual I could not imagine, she related to me her life as an Aboriginal woman growing up in BC, her children taken from her and placed in residential schools, one of whom died of tuberculosis. She told me of the beatings that she suffered at the hands of her partner when alcohol got out of hand, and how the authorities did little or nothing to help. Her cousin had died in a RCMP jail cell from a severe beating. Eye witnesses later told her that while her cousin had been drunk and disorderly, he was in perfect health when put into the police car on that fateful night. Now, she said, self-government and land claims would bring wealth and justice to her people. Now, she said proudly, they could better care for themselves.

I tried to explain that I did not believe that the solution to past failures was to create law that segregates people on the basis of their race. Neither did I believe that simply transferring power from a white police force to an Aboriginal constabulary would provide any guarantee that justice would be done. She wiped her tears away and replied, "You people segregated us already, through the DIA [Department of Indian Affairs] and the Indian Act. At least this way we can tend to our own affairs."

"True," I agreed, "but there are many of us who would like to get rid of that racist piece of legislation and the millions of dollars that are spent in the administration of the Department of Indian Affairs and Northern Resources. The solution, however, is not to create new jurisdictions, where rights, privileges, and authority are exclusive to one's race. I don't wish to discriminate against you. Why would you choose to discriminate against me?" "I gotta get on the bus," she said, rising and not answering my question. Then she added, "Lot of people listen to you, Wilson. You speak from the heart. But I worry about our people. Listen to their cries."

THE IMPORTANCE OF EQUALITY

After she left, I sat for a moment, moved by the telling of her history, but certain that if our children are to live together in peace, harmony, and equality, we must renew our definition of what it is to be Canadian. Whatever our definition, we must establish that every Canadian is equal to every other Canadian. We can no longer divide our people on racial grounds, as we have done in the past, and as we continue to do through the Indian Act. Surely now when so much has been learned through our common history, we will not entrench those divisions in a new constitution. Today's solutions cannot be based on anger or greed. They must be based on an understanding and acceptance of the principles of equality. When so much is at stake, surely we will not let history repeat itself. I offer the above two stories to illustrate the great difficulty that one faces when confronting the question of Aboriginal treaty settlements.

THE REALPOLITIK OF ABORIGINAL LAND CLAIMS

There is no issue currently before the BC government that will have a greater effect on the people of our province than the resolution of First Nations land claims. The impact of these decisions will be profound in two respects: (1) their cost in dollars and (2) their long-term effects with respect to title, and the corresponding jurisdiction that such title will provide to Aboriginal people.

On the first of these, it is clear that we are already well beyond our capacity to handle our provincial and federal debt. We are broke! Consequently, it seems to me most strange that elected politicians continue to entertain the settlement of land claims when they know they lack the financial means with which to settle them. This is made even more strange when we consider that there is no legal obligation to move negotiations along, even though we are told there is a popular mood to settle these matters quickly and fairly.

Remember, however, the fate of the Charlottetown Accord, which was the product of months of laborious negotiations between the provinces and the federal government, and the Aboriginal people. The Accord, like the Meech Lake Agreement before it, was supposed to be the final resolution to Canada's so-called "constitutional crisis", including the question of Aboriginal self-government. Fortunately, the majority of ordinary Canadians, Aboriginal and non-Aboriginal alike, smelled a rat in the Canadian establishment's campaign to stampede them into approving the Accord's all too vague terms in the national referendum of 26 October 1992, and voted against this deal.

CHARLOTTETOWN BY THE BACK DOOR

So why are the federal and provincial governments and representatives of the First Nations busy implementing it in British Columbia today? In fact, BC's NDP government, under Mike Harcourt, began to move toward a recognition of Aboriginal self-government, as set out in the ill-fated Charlottetown Accord, shortly after the Accord was defeated in the referendum by firing the law firm that had successfully argued the Delgamuuth case before Chief Justice McEchern. The new legal team that was hired moved quickly to an appeal that advanced the position that political legitimacy could be given to the concept of "inherent Aboriginal rights to self-government", and that the courts held no authority over this matter. The appeal was upheld, but contrary to what was widely reported in the popular media, the

Court did not reverse the McEchern ruling that Aboriginal title did not exist within the lands in question.

Ronald Irwin, federal Minister of Indian and Northern Affairs, has stated that the "inherent right to self-government" will be implemented within the first four-year term of the current Liberal government to provide First Nations a level of autonomy to manage their own affairs, especially economic development opportunities that currently are handled directly from within the Department of Indian and Northern Affairs. Ironically, just as in the Charlottetown Accord, there is no text of legislation available for Canadians to study that spells out just what "inherent right" means, or what the social, economic, and political implications of such a move will be with respect to ongoing funding of such an initiative. Given the manner in which Chretien handled the proposed changes to provide Quebec a constitutional veto and recognition of its distinct society, Canadians have a right to be concerned.

THE DEPARTMENT OF INDIAN AFFAIRS

When, in 1969 Pierre Elliot Trudeau introduced his white paper on repealing the Indian Act, the loudest cry against this came from the Aboriginal leadership. The reasons are fairly obvious. The annual budgets given most Chiefs and band councils by the Department of Indian Affairs and Northern Resources provide them opportunity to direct those dollars toward projects that occasionally enhance their own investments, or towards people who, within the terms of reference of any government other than Aboriginal, would be in violation of conflict of interest rules.

Recently, I was approached by a young First Nations man, who told me about a consulting group headed up by the brother of the Chief on his reserve, which, within days of its formation, had received a contract from the Chief worth about $75,000. This contract was to advise the band council on a variety of matters, one of which was a policy on nepotism! As if that were not enough to launch the complaint, the man explained that the issue that really concerned him was that this new company had just hired several individuals who currently sit on the band council to help with the project. Needless to say one of the consulting group's first recommendations was to increase the overall amount of the contract.

The most disturbing aspect of this story, however, is that because the money involved came directly from the Department of Indian Affairs and Northern Resources, I began to enquire of officials in the department as to how this sort of thing was possible, but could not, through two days of phoning, find anyone who was prepared to discuss it. I was told that if the band member to whom I had been talking had a complaint, he should take it to his Chief and council! What this story illustrates is the complete lack of accountability that exists with respect to the assignment and administration of dollars from the department to various First Nations bands. From a Canadian taxpayer's point of view, I object to our money being spent in such a manner. The second point that is illustrated by this simple story (and there are many worse examples) is the reason why so many in charge of Indian Bands don't want to change the arrangement that they have with Ottawa. Self-government by all means, but don't stop the supply of money.

To put this in perspective: in the 1995 budget year, the federal government spent $4.5 billion within the Department of Indian Affairs and Northern Development, an additional $3 billion directed specifically toward Aboriginal programs in health, education, and social services, which if added to $1.5 billion in tax concessions, totals $9 billion to provide service to about 600,000 Status Indians within Canada. This translates into roughly $15,000 per man, woman, and child. Yet, if one visits any of the reserves, in British Columbia at least, we find people living in abject poverty. The reason is that a large percentage of the department's budget is spent to support a massive infrastructure of bureaucrats, including lawyers, accountants, and sundry advisors and counsellors. If this continues under Aboriginal self-government, then I fear for the people who will experience it.

ABORIGINAL DIVISIONS

Another critical point is that not all Aboriginal people qualify for the federal money that is spent on their behalf. It is important here to review the distinctions that exist between Aboriginal people themselves. First, there exist Treaty Indians. These are Aboriginal people who hold written treaties with the Crown or its agent. In this case, the terms and conditions of land ownership, rights to resources, and characteristics of the social contract with Canada are spelled out. Second are members of First Nations who are on reserves and "Status" Indians. In their case, the distinguishing characteristic is the fact that they were recognised through the language of the Indian Act by the Crown when the fiduciary responsibility, or government jurisdiction, for Aboriginal people was transferred to the government of Canada. Within the province of British Columbia, these "First Nations" are constituted by any manner acceptable to themselves. It is this group who are primarily involved in the BC Treaty Commission process.

The third group are the non-Status, non-landed Aboriginal people. This group are for the most part urban, and have varied family or racial backgrounds. Included in this third group are the Metis, although they would prefer a special status of their own. The Metis claim a direct spiritual descendency from Louis Riel, and are fiercely proud of their bloodlines. Certainly, they have had a unique history within Canada. For the purpose of this chapter, I will leave out the Metis, although in doing so let me say that I have a full understanding of their particular set of circumstances.

Although, in fact, the situation of a majority of the Metis is not dissimilar to that of the significant percentage of largely urban Aboriginal people who do not live on reserves, and may not be even tied in any way to a particular territory. This group has established a body to represent their concerns called, the United Native Nations, or UNN, through which they demand rights and privileges equal to those of other First Nations. The difficulty with this position lies in the fact that their "inherent rights", if recognized, ultimately must be determined on an individual basis, which the other First Nations argue must be tied to a specific band. Given the degree of interracial union in today's world, bloodlines are often quite confused. It is difficult to see how individuals whose parentage may be mixed through successive generations can claim particular rights that are different from those of their neighbours.

HISTORICAL RIGHTS

The key point here is that throughout Canada's history the Aboriginal people have been treated as wards of the state, but their individual rights, however they are defined, have never been extinguished, and neither have their collective rights. In examining those "rights", however, we must accept that there is no mention anywhere that either individual or collective rights include jurisdiction and title over land, except in the case of a specific treaty signed with a specific Indian band. Further, the Constitution makes no specific mention of Aboriginal people as a distinct part of Canada.

THE CANADA CLAUSE

There are those who argue that such an omission must be corrected, but others will cite the fact that Canada is a country of many cultures, and the inclusion of one group implies the exclusion of every other. During the drafting of the

Charlottetown Accord there was lengthy debate over what became known as the "Canada clause". This clause was written to include the Aboriginal people, along with the two founding nations, the British and the French. Those that remember this debate will recall my solid rejection of any definition that split Canada into three: English Canada, French Canada, and Aboriginal Canada.

RACISM AND FIRST NATIONS CITIZENSHIP

With the transfer of so much power into the hands of the band Chief and council, consideration has to be given to the protection of the individual. This becomes critical when one understands that our federal and provincial governments today are prepared to grant various First Nations bands the right to decide, without appeal to the courts, who their "citizens" are under this new governmental structure. This concept is as bizarre a notion to me as having a Quebec separatist party as the Loyal Opposition in Ottawa.

For example, the agreement that was signed between the Nisga'a, the province of BC and the government of Canada on the matter of citizenship in 1995 states that the determination of Nisga'a citizenship, with all of the rights that such citizenship confers, will be determined by two members from each of the four Nisga'a clan groups on the basis of the mother's kin-line. Should a person not agree with their decision, she or he will have the right to appeal to a board composed of two Nisga'a appointed by the Nisga'a government and one senior federal civil servant appointed by Ottawa. There will be no appeal available to the courts of Canada, because they will hold no jurisdiction over the matter!

The granting of "membership" or "citizenship" within First Nations provides for an entrenchment of the "Aboriginal status" spelled out in the Indian Act. The only difference now is that eligibility will rest with the First Nations people themselves. Under the laws of Canada, Aboriginal people will be seen to be distinct people, separate from mainstream, multicultural Canadian society. Yet there is no provision within the law to discriminate against Aboriginal people in terms of their status as Canadian citizens. What will result from this practice is the creation of a new class of citizen who will enjoy exclusive benefits provided by virtue of his or her membership within a particular First Nation, as well as all of the benefits provided a non-Aboriginal Canadian.

The obvious conflict that can arise from this practice is at the root of my concern. Whenever a country openly discriminates, there are problems. When a country openly legislates such discrimination, the country itself is in peril. The very nature of citizenship, and the egalitarianism that has opened Canada to immigrants from all over the world, allows people to choose to be part of our society. No matter what the bloodline, once citizenship is granted, we are equal. But under the terms of the proposed Nisga'a agreement for example, if I am not born Nisga'a, I can never be

Nisga'a. Thus, the benefits that go with the land are exclusive to the Nisga'a. This practice is by any definition, discriminatory and thus racist.

The implications of this agreement are so numerous and so profound that it is impossible to cover them all here. The bottom line, however, is quite clear. These changes will re-define our country, and create some new entity where race is a factor in one's rights, and where language and culture may be used to entrench the rights of one group over those of another. I will leave it to the reader to consider the consequences.

INDIVIDUAL AND COLLECTIVE RIGHTS

The final matter that requires some thought is that for many First Nations the prescription of individual rights, especially as they apply to equality between men and women, are quite foreign and thus unacceptable. I can recall, for example, a discussion that I had with Chief Archie Jack of the Penticton Band in 1992 after the vote on the Charlottetown Accord. He made quite clear to me that his Band would never accept the Canadian Charter of Rights, because the notion of Charter equality ran counter to the historical relationship between men and women.

Similarly, the concept of the individual ownership of land is a concept that is completely foreign to Aboriginal people. In his book *Maps and Dreams*, Hugh Brody, in examining the complex pattern of land use that took place in the northern regions of this country, provides much insight into the problems that are encountered when we try to lay a western system of land tenure over the historical territories of First Nations people. The historical patterns of Aboriginal land use were tied to the family trap lines, which were determined by the winter and summer hunting patterns. Unlike a western map of land tenure, where there would be a grid pattern outlining plots or hectares of privately owned land, the map of the northern Aboriginal people looked more like a series of lines crisscrossing the land. These lines marked the journey from one trap to another, and to the uninitiated would look more like the scribbles of a preschooler than what they really represent, which is generations of land use representing each family's historic claim to the land.

LAND CLAIMS

The argument that ownership existed, however, is very much a part of the land negotiations that are now underway. The Aboriginal leadership argue that the collective interest of First Nations people is best served if they are able to carve out a territory, draw lines around it on a modern map, and thus define that land as "traditional territory". In large measure that has already been done, at least in part, with the establishment of Indian Reserves. However, the amount of land defined within the reserves is only a fraction of what is now being claimed as part of the comprehensive land claims process.

Any first year political geography student will tell you

that extravagant land claims are not unique to the Aboriginal people. One of the most basic assumptions made by any who seek autonomy, either as a budding nation state or within a nation state, is control if not outright sovereignty over its territory. The territorial imperative is fundamental to a nation state. Canada, the actual nation state within which this disputed land exists, must now find ways to distinguish the legitimate claims made regarding lands previously alienated from First Nations people from those that are made purely to advance the interests of a new Aboriginal elite within Canada, or to advance notions of First Nations sovereignty. Anything that diminishes the sovereignty of the federal government over its territory is completely unacceptable.

SPECIAL STATUS

It is interesting to observe that when we come to the matter of Quebec independence, the leadership in Quebec holds a similar point of view to that of the Aboriginal leadership, with one major exception. Successive governments in Quebec, both separatist and nationalist, have consistently argued the two nation theory, namely that Canada is made up of two founding nations, English and French. From that point forward they argue that because Quebec enjoys a system of French civil law, as opposed to British common law, because Quebec has a majority of French speaking inhabitants, and a defined territory with a distinct boundary, that they should have special status within Canada.

Consider how similar the Aboriginal and Quebec government positions are. Both argue for special status based on a premise that Canada is still the product of its colonial history and, therefore, despite nearly 130 years of growth and change, we must make modern decisions based on historical records that they cite. Rather than spend time challenging their dubious arguments, I believe that it is more important to question the relevance of the debate over special rights and privileges. We live at a time in human history when we are quickly entering into a modern North American economy, influenced by rapid changes in the global economy, and driven by a sophisticated communications technology that links people around the world in a blink of an eye.

RESOURCE ALLOCATION

There is an additional element to this discussion, and that is the right to resources, both above and below the land, and migratory living resources such as fish and game. In this matter, the position taken by most First Nations people is that there must be compensation for past uses of the resources, and until this matter is cleared up, there should not be any further harvesting of resources without their contractual agreement. These so called "joint stewardship agreements" have become the norm in many areas with respect to forestry activity, but are now under discussion with respect to mining as well.

On the matter of the West Coast fishery, there has been a different approach, with a very liberal interpretation by federal bureaucrats of the ruling handed down in what is now commonly called the Sparrow decision. That ruling provided First Nations people the right to catch salmon for subsistence and ceremonial purposes. There was no mention of a commercial fishery. Neither did this ruling provide for the buying and selling of fish. Yet, after this ruling, the federal Department of Fisheries implemented the Aboriginal Fish Strategy, which has had a significant negative impact on the West Coast fishery. There are no barriers specific to Aboriginal people who wish to enter into the commercial fishery, and indeed there are many who have been, and continue to be, very successful. Why, then, do we need a new classification where eligibility to participate is determined by racial origin?

THE TREATY COMMISSION PROCESS

In 1993, the provincial and federal governments signed an agreement with the First Nations to establish a Treaty Commission to assist Aboriginal groups to prepare for and enter into negotiations on their land claims. The Treaty Commission is now the only process by which land claims can be settled, and it is meeting with some success in some quarters, while in others, particularly with the interior bands, the Commission has not done well.

There is no doubt that the issue of self-government is key to the success of all final negotiations over land. To that end, the British Columbia government should make as a pre-condition to future land negotiations the repeal of the

Indian Act, the abolition of the Department of Indian Affairs and Northern Resources, and the immediate establishment of self-government over the reserve lands that are not contested. Until such government is in place, and there is a demonstration of success of such a government within a democratic framework, negotiations should not proceed further. There are a few such examples already, the Sechelts being the best, where successful self-government has existed for almost a decade. This gives me reason to hope that the negotiations that are taking place now to settle a comprehensive land claim may well benefit all of the people who live within the Sechelt Inlet area, and not just the Sechelt First Nation.

If we are to be successful, however, we must be rigid in our defence of the democratic process, and the inclusion of the protections that are provided within the Charter of Rights and Freedoms. We must also resist the kind of policies that provide for an open discrimination against or in favour of one group within our society. The establishment of the Aboriginal Fish Strategy and its fundamental premise of rights on the basis of race is an example of such an approach, and it should be abandoned. Clearly, there are historic Aboriginal rights that must be accepted and adhered to, but by the same token, those rights must be read in the context of the larger social contract that we, as Canadians, have with each other.

As we proceed to establish Aboriginal self-government, it is imperative that all enabling legislation provide that Aboriginal communities be governed by the Criminal Code, and be subjected to the same provincial statues as other forms of municipal governance. One of the first tests of this rule will undoubtedly come with the introduction of for-profit gambling. There are currently at least eight Bands who are working toward the introduction of Las Vegas-style casinos. In 1994, the Harcourt government plans for a casino in Vancouver brought forth such a storm of public protest that the government backed away from the idea. The point is that the government's proposal would have required a change in provincial law, and in the federal Criminal Code. The question is, when the new Gaming Act finally becomes law (as it is certain to do) will it apply equally to the First Nations as it does to all other British Columbians? Certainly, up until the appointment of the new Attorney General, Ujjal Dosanjh, there appeared to be two laws contemplated.

The ultimate irony in all of this is that many of us who argue for equality for every Canadian, with no special status for any group, are often branded as racists. Nothing could be further from the truth. The fact is that a full and proper public debate on the whole First Nations land claims/self-government question is long overdue. If we believe in this country, and in this province as a strong and equal partner in a renewed Confederation, then it is time that we stood firm on principle. We must challenge those who would divide this country into jurisdictions where individual rights are defined by one's race, and where equality of opportunity does not exist.

APPENDIX
THE NISGA'A SETTLEMENT

At this short notice, I can do no better than to present my readers with three of my "Wilson's Weekly" columns from the *Powell River News* on the subject of the Nisga'a Agreement in Principle. I think you will find my position consistent with the broad views presented in the final chapter of this book.

FEBRUARY 13, 1996

There was considerable jubilation amongst those who had been closeted behind closed doors putting together the final language of an agreement between the Nisga'a and the federal and provincial governments. Chief Joe Gosnell came out from the meeting and declared that "The journey our forefathers began well over a century ago ended this morning." Well, I hope so, because there is a real need for a just and fair settlement in this and every other outstanding claim, and at first reading of the agreement there is much in it which is good. But, there are critical details missing from the text that has been released, especially with respect to fishing and mining regulations. Without those details, there are a few miles to travel yet.

Despite openness in some of the meetings that have taken place that has provided for locally elected officials to attend along with some members of the general public, the people of British Columbia are for the most part unaware of what the government has negotiated with the Nisga'a on their behalf in terms of the future relationship between Nisga'a people and the rest of us. We must have those details now, before there is a signature on the documents that will put in place an agreement that will bind future generations for decades to come.

Aboriginal Affairs Minister John Cashore said on Tuesday morning that the text of the agreement would be available to any who wish to review it, and there would be a series of public hearings to provide an opportunity for those who feel their interest is affected to have their say. I welcome that approach as it is consistent with the approach that I put to the Minister two weeks ago. But, we must be clear as to what the public hearings are about, and the degree to which those public hearings will constitute further negotiation.

There is a great deal made about the $190 million that has been proposed as cash up front, and to be sure in a country that is over $700 billion in debt, that has to be a consideration. As citizens living in a province of roughly three million people, and a debt of over $28 billion, when our schools are being amalgamated with services cut, and our hospitals facing greater reduction in funding, we have a right to know what our direct share will be. Remember that there is only one tax payer.

From the Nisga'a point of view, however, after over one hundred of years of alienation, and over twenty years of direct negotiation, they want to settle their claim. Who could blame them? It is for that reason that the position taken by the Liberal Opposition is so offensive. With Campbell's statement that he reserves the right to throw out the deal and negotiate again, what he is in effect suggesting is that the parties should go ahead and sign a deal, but should he not like it, he will reserve the authority to throw it out.

That approach will simply not work. A negotiated treaty must be binding on all parties, and it must be a final settlement. British Columbians do not want to have to constantly be re-negotiating on these agreements. When the deal is struck, it had better be fair to all people, and had better not bind us to on going funding through a simple transfer of power over the Indian Act from the federal government to a Nisga'a self-government.

If one party reserves the right to open up the deal any time it is politically opportune for them to do so, then we will be no further ahead. No, a deal must be final, and while minor issues will need to be addressed on an ongoing basis, the text of an agreement must be such that the new relationship is binding.

It is for this reason that I so strongly believe that the process used to ratify any agreement must be open to all British Columbians, and must include the detailed text of the agreement. Governments at all levels must stop thinking that they know best, and that somehow the people should be shielded from the details of this agreement. Those lessons were learned during the process that surrounded the Meech Lake Agreement and the Charlottetown Accord.

For my part, I am less concerned with the total dollars spent, although that is important, than I am with the model of self-government that is put in place. The biggest issue is one of governance, and the powers that a Nisga'a government will have with respect to not only the Nisga'a people, but all British Columbians, especially over the management of resources that are currently open to all citizens.

What I will be looking for in the Nisga'a agreement will be the powers that the Nisga'a First Nations will have over their territory, and the extent to which they will be empowered to access their resource base in an exclusive manner. I will also want to look at the language of the agreement to make sure that it is not discriminatory in its intent.

For years aboriginal people have been shackled by the Indian Act, let's hope that whatever is in this agreement does not simply transfer the authority from the Act to a new government that will still be empowered to institute discrimination on the basis of race, culture, or language.

This agreement must be seen with optimistic eyes, because I believe all Canadians want to make sure that a just settlement is ratified. But, be forewarned. The detail of this agreement must not entrench special rights, jurisdiction and privilege for one group over all others, without reference to the Canadian Constitution and the Charter of

Rights. What is before us is encouraging in this respect, however, there are many questions to be answered with respect
to citizenship, and a parallel set of laws and judiciary.

The text of this agreement introduces a new concept
within our democracy, that of dual citizenship, where citizenship is defined on the basis of race. There are also powers that are provided to those who hold that citizenship, and
as such the language is inherently discriminatory. The docu-
ment is also ambiguous with respect to the powers of Nisga'a
government over non-Nisga'a who live within their land.
Both of these concepts are dangerous, because they open
the door to a precedent where race is a determining factor
to one's rights.

While the celebrations continue, there is much within
this agreement that will need to be clearly understood before a final ratification will be accepted by those of us, Aboriginal and non-Aboriginal who are not Nisga'a.

FEBRUARY 27, 1996

This week's column is devoted to an explanation and critique
of the "Agreement in Principle" that was signed between the
Nisga'a, Province of B.C. and Canada. I have deliberately
not made substantive comment on the agreement until such
time as I had studied the text available and availed myself of
the negotiators who put the deal together to have what questions I had, and there were many, answered.

It is important at the outset to say that the text that has
been put before us for comment is not a final agreement.

There are many issues that are to be negotiated before such a final agreement can take place, and they are important issues that will impact such matters as taxation authority, administration of justice, and future financing agreements. So the text of this agreement in principle is not the final deal. It does, however, set out a clear framework within which the final details are to be discussed.

I have long said that in order for treaties to be negotiated with some finality they must be based upon those lands that are undisputed, the reserves, and that those reserves should be declared First Nations territory. I have also said that a form of self-government should be established over those territories that does not entrench in the Canadian Constitution the right to discriminate on the basis of race. This agreement meets that test.

On the question of land, the Nisga'a Nation will collectively hold fee simple title to their existing reserve lands that amounts to roughly 1,930 square km in the lower Nass Valley. As owners in fee simple, they will be able to trade on their land, and borrow against it just as you or I might do on land that we own. The important point here is that the residual title of that land rests with the Crown in perpetuity. No sovereign status, or anything even close to it.

The agreement also provides that legally vested real property interests on Nisga'a Lands such as rights of way, easements, licenses and permits that provide for such things as Hydro transmission lines, telephone lines, water supply, gas pipelines and roads will be continued by Nisga'a Government in accordance with their terms that exist on the effective date of this agreement. In layman's language, those rights of way must be continued in perpetuity as long as they continue to be used for the purpose they were constructed. No blockades, no preventing access. And because they must be maintained within existing terms, financial levies on those rights of way stay the same.

As to the matter of self-government, those who know me will have heard me say over and over, "every Canadian equal under the law to every other Canadian regardless of race". I stand by that, and I think this agreement does also. There are three important aspects to this agreement in principle that gives me a great deal of hope that we will make a fair and just settlement with the Aboriginal people in B.C. without balkanizing Canada into a few dozen homelands.

First, and most important, this agreement is made within the framework of the Canadian constitution. "The *Canadian Charter of Rights and Freedoms* will apply to Nisga'a Government and its institutions in relation to all matters within its jurisdiction and authority . . ." and further "laws of general application will apply to Nisga'a citizens and on Nisga'a Lands . . ." and lastly, "Federal and provincial laws will apply to Nisga'a citizens and to Nisga'a Lands . . ." within the context of the treaty rights that are spelled out in a final agreement. So quite clearly this is not a "third order of government" as contemplated in the Charlottetown Accord. Neither is it a government that is parallel to the province, and in matters of environmental standards, land use and resource extraction, the provincial laws such as the forest practices code, the environmental review process apply.

The second important point is that this agreement will be considered exhaustive in terms of the Nisga'a peoples inherent rights. In other words once this deal is done, the "inherent rights" of the Nisga'a people will be clearly defined, and not, as is the case now, undefined and up to the courts to determine. This agreement provides that "eventually the *Indian Act* will no longer apply to the Nisga'a Nation and its people." With that agreement, the federal and provincial tax exemption will no longer apply, and the Nisga'a will be treated in terms of their taxation just like you or me.

The third important point is that the agreement provides for appeal to the Canadian court system, either provincial in the case of civil litigation, or federal in terms of the criminal code. Even though this agreement will provide for a Nisga'a court, that court must be established much like any other regional court, and must be approved by, and governed under, the provincial and federal statues.

The matter of non-Nisga'a representation within government is an important point to raise also. I have always said that there can be no taxation without representation, and once again this agreement will in the final text, I believe, meet that test. While it is true that no non-Nisga'a can run for office on the Central Government, it is equally true that the Nisga'a government cannot pass laws that effect non-Nisga'a people. They can however pass land-use regulations that will effect those who are lease holders on Nisga'a Land. I don't have too much trouble with that aspect, because it is very much like being a tenant within a strata title complex. The owners have the right to decide what they want to do with the building, and as a tenant you have some protection under the law to protect your interests, but you don't have a right to make the decision with owners. That is the same in this agreement.

Any right of taxation cannot be entered into without first full, and quite onerous consultation with those that will be affected, and taxation must fall within the "laws of general application". So a non-Nisga'a who is taxed has the right to representation through the provincial government and will have the right to appeal just as you do now, through an appeal process.

In areas where non-Nisga'a may be directly affected such as school boards, hospital boards and so on, the non-Nisga'a do have a right to hold office, and to vote. That is a major step in the right direction, and one that I fully support.

So, is this a good deal? Well yes for the most part, but not in the area of the fishery. I strongly disagree with entrenching within the Constitution a commercial right to any individual or group, and this agreement does that. The Constitution provides for individual and collective rights within the framework of the law, it should not be used to entrench in perpetuity a commercial share of any resource. This is a very dangerous precedent to make, and could lead us down a very dangerous path.

Next week, I will discuss the Fishery aspect in detail, and will outline my concerns with both the text and the appended agreement. In the meantime, I urge you to get a copy of the agreement either through my office on Marine

Ave, or through the Government Agent and read it. This is an important treaty, and one that will affect the outcome of many other agreements to follow.

MARCH 05, 1996

Last week I wrote about the agreement in principle between the Nisga'a and the federal and provincial governments. As you may have read, I was generally supportive of this agreement in principle because it met the three major tests that I felt needed to be addressed. The agreement was governed within the context of the Canadian constitution, the Charter of Rights and Freedoms prevails, and there is no provision for Nisga'a government to subjugate the laws of Canada or British Columbia. For greater certainty, the residual title to the land remained with the Crown. I did, however, take exception to the section of this agreement in principle that deals with fish. This week, I would like to explain why.

The section of this agreement that deals with fish should be read in two parts. Those rights that are within the agreement and will therefore be considered Treaty Rights, and the additional guarantees that are provided for in a separate agreement that will not be entrenched within the Constitution. It is to the first part that I have the biggest problem.

Let me state clearly, I do not support the position that any individual, or group of individuals, collective or corporation should have within the Canadian Constitution a guarantee to a commercial share of a resource. The Canadian constitution provides for certain guarantees that affect the general quality of life of our citizens, it provides certain guarantees with respect to our freedoms, to speech, to assembly, to live without discrimination, but it does not now, nor should it ever, provide a right to a commercial share of a resource. This agreement provides such a guarantee.

The basis for this guarantee is linked to the First Nations claim to a right to salmon as part of their historical relationship with the land, and their social customs that are built around that relationship. The right to harvest salmon for ceremonial and subsistence has been tested in the courts, and the courts have ruled that there does exist an inherent right to a "food fishery". This was dealt with most specifically in a court ruling that upheld the rights of an aboriginal man, Charlie Sparrow who was charged under the Fisheries Act for illegally taking salmon. The court ruled that Sparrow had a right to the fish for subsistence and for ceremonial purposes.

The difficulty with this issue arose when the federal Department of Fisheries and Oceans took the "Sparrow ruling" and interpreted the judgment to include the selling of those fish that were caught as "food fish". They further complicated the issue when they introduced the Aboriginal Fish Strategy which amended the licensing practice and harvest limits to fish for Aboriginal people, especially within the Fraser River system. I argue that while there is an inherent right to fish for subsistence and ceremonial purposes, the

141

moment that those fish are exchanged for money, that is commerce, and should be treated as part of the commercial fishery.

What this agreement provides for in any year where the number of species of Nass salmon returning to Canadian waters, less incidental harvests, is greater than the minimum escapement level determined by the federal Minister of Fisheries and Oceans, the Nisga'a people will be entitled to harvest a number of each of the five species of salmon with a guaranteed minimum, and established maximum. This guarantee will effectively constitute an entitlement to the resource and will be spelled out within the final agreement, and thus be constitutionally binding.

If this guarantee was restricted only to those fish that would be domestically consumed, or used for ceremonial purposes, then the only argument would be the numbers of salmon that would be harvested. But this agreement in principle does not restrict the Nisga'a who harvest fish under this guarantee, from selling their fish through a cash market. Hence, we have just entrenched a commercial guarantee into the Canadian Constitution.

Some will argue that this is a small price to pay for an otherwise good deal, others will argue that historically the Nisga'a were able to barter or trade their fish, so "what's the real difference here?" To those points I respond that if this were the only entitlement to fish that was provided for that perhaps, just perhaps, we might find accommodation for the offensive clause, but it is not. In addition to this guarantee, the Nisga'a will "establish management regimes for aboriginal, commercial and recreational salmon fisheries, such as the development of harvest quotas, to ensure the viability of such fisheries." The agreement goes on to say "The form of Nisga'a salmon entitlements may be made compatible with such management regimes, with the agreement of Nisga'a Central Government."

This regime will be governed by a harvest agreement that is set outside of the Canadian Constitution Act, 1982, and is in addition to the treaty rights that are protected within the Constitution. The harvest allocation is specific by species, with Sockeye equivalent to 13% of the adjusted Total Allowable Catch, Pinks equivalent to 15% of the adjusted TAC, and so on.

There are also provisions for the harvest of "surplus" salmon, along with the ability to average the harvest entitlement should there be lean years where the harvest is under the prescribed minimum. In addition to those fish, the Nisga'a will be entitled to harvest Chinook, Coho and Chum salmon that are identified as resulting from Nisga'a enhancement initiatives, provided that they are surplus to spawning requirements, and match the Nisga'a share of that investment.

On the last point, one could argue that it is only fair that if money is spent enhancing a stock, those who invest should benefit from it. I have no argument with that point, except that the federal government is advancing $11.5 million to the Nisga'a Central Government to enable it to increase its capacity in the coast-wide commercial fishery.

So what is the solution to this inherently dangerous

precedent? In my view the solution is to provide a constitutional right to only those fish that will be domestically consumed, or used for ceremonial purposes and not allow the sale of any of those fish that are harvested under a constitutional guarantee.

Having done that, provide by separate agreement the Nisga'a with 15 percent of the commercial fishing licenses, and let them compete for the stock just like anyone else. Let the good fishers survive and restore some fairness to an industry that is over administered, and in desperate need of support. In essence there is only one fishery not four, and it is important that this agreement not entrench within our constitution the lines that have been created between aboriginal, commercial, recreational, and conservation fisheries as they have been allowed to develop under current policy from the federal government.

This is a critical issue, and one that will not go away. The solution that I propose I believe is a fair one. It will provide the necessary stability within the fishery, it will provide a fair opportunity for the Nisga'a to fully participate in the commercial fishery, and will respect their inherent right to a resource for personal consumption and ceremonial use. I hope over the course of the next few months such a solution can be seriously discussed.